Local Narratives, Global Media

Local Narratives, Global Media:

Regional Television Stations and the use of New Communications Technologies in Himalayan, India

Abdul Nasir Khan

GYAN

First Published, 2018

Published by

Gyan Publishing House
5, Ansari Road
Daryaganj, New Delhi-110002
Phone: 9811692060
E-mail: books@gyanbooks.com

Printed at: G. Print Process, Delhi.

Cataloging in Publication Data—DK
Courtesy: D.K. Agencies (P) Ltd. <docinfo@dkagencies.com>

Khan, Abdul Nasir, author.
Local narratives, global media : regional television stations and the use of new communications technologies in Himalayan, India / Abdul Nasir Khan.
pages cm
Includes bibliographical references.
ISBN 9788121214223 (HB)

1. Local mass media—India—Kargil. 2. Television broadcasting of news—India—Kargil. 3. Mass media—Social aspects—India—Kargil. 4. Online social networks—India—Kargil—Influence. I. Title.

LCC P96.L622K37 2018 | DDC 302.2309546 23

Contents

Preface

When I was very young I had no idea about television; no one that we knew in Ladakh, a region in Himalayan India, had one. Elders in the town often used to listen to news and cricket commentaries on the radio. Then suddenly one day I started hearing that rather than listening to the news some people were watching the news, with pictures and videos in the stories, on the television. It sounded like magic.

I clearly remember the first time I watched television in late 1984. It was the funeral procession for Prime Minister Indira Gandhi. All India Radio (AIR) had a station in Leh, and the government-owned channel Doordarshan, which at the time was in the same department as AIR, was establishing a small office there. Since my father worked at AIR we were invited with a small group of people to watch the funeral on a television set up in the courtyard outside of their office. A tarp was spread on the ground and about 50 of us sat and watched it. It was unbelievable to see the live telecast; I was amazed to think that I was watching what was happening in Delhi – a place I had never been—at the same time it was happening there.

Slowly television worked its way into our homes, and we had our own at my house. It was a sign of prestige and wealth, and I was proud to invite my friends to see it. Doordarshan was the only channel available. For first few months of television viewing I was simply mesmerised by the combination of images and sound. But slowly a curiosity grew in me, a desire to see my small Himalayan home town on television. I waited months, watching news of unfamiliar places, then one day the moment came when I was able to see Ladakh on the television. It was about a political leader's visit to the region, in a news report that was only couple of minutes long. I was glad to see my town on the television, but I was also disappointed it was very brief. After watching television for few years I began to realise that the programmes were more about people who lived in big cities and towns. It didn't reflect my reality. Thus, growing up I felt that it was impossible to address local issues on television. There is no way a single channel can discuss the issues associated with every town and village in a big country like India.

The explosion of cable television in India in the 1990s changed this; suddenly there was a way for people living in remote parts of India to address their issues. While cable had great potential it also came with its own set of problems. Many of the so-called "local television stations" that started popping up all over India during this time did not address local issues; they commonly were movie channels with rudimentary local business advertisements. The promise of local cable television was further challenged by the rise of the internet in our region in the 2000s, when video-sharing websites and social media became the fastest and cheapest means to disperse the local news and information.

It is in this media setting that I became fascinated with the ways in which the Kargili local media people have used the combination of cable television and social media to start a group of local television stations. As I will discuss in this book, these stations produce news for local consumption, but also provide a national platform for regional issues, and a global network for members of the Kargili diasporas, or anyone else who is interested in the region, around the world.

In the course of my communications studies I have been able to observe how useful local television stations can become for small communities, whether it be for native tribes living in North America or small villages in a remote region of the Himalayas. This information should be shared globally; local responses to media challenges can become a blueprint for others who want to do the same and need some examples. I started researching about the local television stations in Kargil during my undergraduate studies in communications as a personal curiosity; with encouragement from my professors and the community members the research ended up becoming my master's thesis. In the course of this research I have collected lot of information about local television stations, including a case study of Kargili local television stations, a survey of television audiences, and interviews with both audience members and station owners.

There are a lot of different ways of defining local television stations. Some definitions focus on language use, while others focus on regional distribution patterns; there is no one right answer or universal definition of a local television station as it can mean different things for different communities. In this book I discuss these ideas, challenges of running a local television station, and the purpose these stations serve. I consider a question on many people's minds: is there any future for local television stations in a world where all kinds of news can be sent by a smart phone and reach to millions of people around the globe in minutes? I will address this question in the Kargili context by exploring the links between various media technologies. Readers of this book will find out how local television stations evolved in general in India, and particularly in Kargil (Ladakh). The data in this book will help activists, policy-makers, and media outlet owners to understand how local television stations function as media institutions in small communities, detailing how the constant adoption of new technologies can allow local stations to expand, even on a shoestring budget.

Acknowledgements

The author wishes to express sincere gratitude to Dr Fred Fejes, Dr Chris Scodari, and Professor Shane Eason of Florida Atlantic University for all of their guidance and support during the writing of the first version of this manuscript. He would also like to thank all of the professors and staff members at FAU who helped him along the way.

The author is grateful to the following individuals for contributing to this study, including Anayat Ali Shotopa (Correspondent, All India Radio Kargil), Basharat Hussain Ladakhi (Cameraman, Kargil Today; Correspondent India TV), Gulzar Hussain Munshi, Ghulam Nabi Zeya (News reporter, ETV Urdu), Hussain Khalo (Editor-in-Chief/Owner, Kargil Today), Mohd Ali Wahid, Nasir Hussain (Director/ Owner, S TV Ladakh), Noor Ul Islam (Owner, Al Noor News Network Ladakh), Sajjad Hussain (Correspondent, Sahar Urdu TV), and Zakir Sengey. He would also like to thank all the anonymous participants of the survey for their contributions.

Last but not least, the author wishes to thank Dr Jacqueline Fewkes, Mr Ramzan Khan, Ms Attiya Kousar, Ms Rubina Kousar, Mr Abdul Rauf, Mr Abdul Mateen, Adil Rauf, Tasneem Rauf, Arjumand Rauf, Amina Khan, and Zayd Khan.

Chapter - 1

Discovering Local Media

A few years ago I was searching the internet to find news and information about a road accident in the small Himalayan town of Kargil in northern India. I found that only a couple of state media outlets had included the accident's story on their websites, with basic information that lacked detail. While it is understandable that it is almost impossible for the Indian national media to cover the thousands of accidents that must happen every day in the country, or even regional media to cover everything happening in a large state like Jammu and Kashmir, this was disappointing. However, during my research a web link in an internet search engine opened a story about the accident, in a YouTube news video that had all the important information. After further research I found several other videos of cultural events, local politics, development issues, and affairs of the small town, all produced by local cable television stations. These videos resembled contemporary cable news shows produced all over the world and the videos were being distributed internationally, yet their main focus was on only this small community in Kargil.

For me this incident raised many questions about the existence and significance of local television stations, questions that, if answered, may provide us with insights into larger media issues. Considering if these stations serve the interests of local communities, and if so how, can help indicate how certain forms of media become successful. Understanding how they can compete with better funded national and international media corporations may provide insights into how people choose their media.

The purpose of this research is to learn more about the role of local media in the form of regional cable television stations in the Kargil district of the Ladakh region in India. The town of Kargil is one of the two main urban areas in the Ladakh region of state of Jammu and Kashmir in northern India. In these towns, particularly in Kargil, a few local television stations seem to have become a popular alternative to national and transnational channels. The intent of this study is to clarify these roles to understand why local media are very popular only in some areas in the region, and how this is related to contemporary community practices and beliefs. As I will discuss in more detail in the next chapter, a number of authors in communications studies have written about the significance of local television channels for minority and/or regional identity and to address regional concerns (e.g. Higgins, 1999, p. 55; King and Mele, 1999; Meadows, 2009). There is some literature that suggests this is also the case in other parts of India as well (Roy, 2008; Sinclair, 2005). My research question is therefore, is the success of local media in Kargil truly a result of fulfilling the needs and desires of the local community in a way that larger national and transnational media outlets fail to do?

To understand this issue and answer the question I investigate the circumstances through which the first local media stations in Kargil were developed, develop an understanding of the communities associated with these sites, asses the contents of the news on these channels, and gather individual stories about the impact of this regional media in Kargil.

As the internet has become more popular; some communications researchers ask if the internet is replacing local television as a medium through which smaller groups can share their interests and viewpoints (Chen, Funk, Straubhaar, and Spence, 2013). My research will advance knowledge in the communications field about all of these issues, adding to knowledge about the impact of different forms of media; the international case study will allow for me to examine whether the previously claimed roles of local television are universal or not. My primary focus is on locally oriented media in the Kargil region in northern India, however for comparison and contrast I have looked at the information about local television stations in other parts of South Asia and the world.

The main body of research for this book was conducted before 2016. While some or all the local television stations that were used in the book might not work currently, or have changed the way they work, this study captures a crucial moment in the birth and development of these media institutions. Thus, this research also acts as a document of media history, to show how Kargili media has developed, even as the different platforms used by the local stations for sharing news might change.

Television and Broadcasting in India

There are a few reasons why India is an important place to study television issues. First, there has been a rapid expansion of television stations in India within the past few decades; the country went from having just one television station to having thousands in a very short time. Second, the role of media in India is significant because of its global presence; India is one of the largest democratic countries, the second most populated country in the world, and has hundreds of different religious practices and languages spoken. As author S. D. McDowell noted in his article on the impact of globalisation on Indian television policies, whatever broadcasting services and policies are made in India effects the one-fifth of the world's population (McDowell, 1997, p. 152). Not only does India have one of the highest numbers of television viewers in the world, it also exports its television programmes to many other countries.

The history of broadcasting in India starts with radio, which provided a model for broadcasting when television was later introduced in India. In an article on village radio broadcasting during the colonial period in India author J. Zivin gives a historical view of local media in India. Zivin explains that the foundation for media in India comes from the 1930s colonial concept of using radio as a way to "uplift" villagers in rural areas, the "true" Indians (Zivin, 1998). By distinguishing between the rural majority and politicised urban majority, and saying the rural population needed to be uplifted, the British were using media to show, and make sure, that India was not ready for self rule. The switch to a nationally focused media approach only came later as the British "prepared" India for independence. Thus, Zivin suggests that locally focused media and specialised regional programming in local languages was an imperialist tool, developed to support colonial rule (Zivin, 1998).

The history of broadcasting in India after independence suggests that broadcasting remained a divisive issue in the newly independent nation of India. This similarity is not incidental; as Sanjay Asthana writes, the newly independent Indian government used broadcasting, among other tools, as it, "reproduced the colonial state's administrative habits and procedures to realise progress and development in the name of nation-building" (Asthana, 2013, p. 521). A. Singhal *et. al.* write in an article about the spread of television within India that the regular broadcasting of television did not start until 1965; before that in 1959 it was introduced only in Delhi as an experimental educational service (Singhal, Doshi, Rogers and Rahman, 1988, p. 224). American sources of the time period considered this lack of national telecommunications system an impediment to progress and the democratic development of independent India (Bonner, 1959).

In 1975, India used a loaned satellite from United States National Aeronautics and Space Administration (NASA). This made India the first country in entire world to broadcast television on large-scale from space (Bhalla, James and Stevens, 1984).

Purnima Mankekar writes that even before the national television audience existed, however, the viewership was being carefully constructed through government programmes and marketing strategies; in the case of Doordarshan one of the multiple ways a "national audience" was constructed was through state policy (Mankekar, 1999, p. 55). There is a general consensus among television historians that in the beginning Indian television was supposed to show programmes associated with rural education. However, studies showed the unpopularity of these programmes. In Bhalla *et al.* a chart that shows ratings for the different types of programmes on Doordarshan in the 1980s clearly shows this. The chart in the source displays the percentage of televisions switched on for the type of programme listed (Bhalla *et al.,* 1984). "Films and Entertainment Programmes" had 70-80 per cent viewership, while the Doordarshan rural programme (Krishi Darshan), which was broadcast in the evening when most of the people were at home, only had a 2-4 per cent viewership. This was lower than other informative programs such as "Magazine Programme on Science" (29 per cent), "English News Program" (13-15 per cent), and "Documentary on Development Themes (10 per cent). Despite the Government of India's emphasis on using television as a medium for education, large numbers of television viewers were keen to use it as a source of entertainment. The first viewers of television in India were apparently not the intended viewers of development programmes. These early television programmes limited television effects to privileged groups of people living in urban areas.

Although during the early years of television in India there were programmes about the rural Indians, most of whom were farmers, television stations were only located and broadcast in the areas of a few of big cities in India. Most of the villagers did not have access to televisions. As A. N. Chatterjee explains in an article that outlines how community television began in India.

> In 1975, [television broadcasting] was extended to other urban areas such as Mumbai, Chennai and Kolkata,

although the majority of population lived in rural India. Ironically, the state's focus on educational potential of television meant that several of its programmes were rural-oriented when majority of the viewers were city dwellers (Chatterjee, 2012, p. 230).

Showing this scripted version of rural India was directly adopted from the colonial concept of educating rural population through radio and television, and broadcasting became a medium for the ruling party in India to show its urban population that everything was going smoothly in Indian villages, a way of placating the masses. A study done in the later part of 1970s showed that while approximately 24 per cent of the government channel viewers were poor and illiterate about 25 per cent of people living in rural areas did not use any kind of media at all (Bhalla *et al.,* 1984). Another study during the same time affirmed that majority of the rural population did not have enough leisure time to watch television at all (Bhalla *et al.,* 1984).

Early Indian television was an educational tool; Mankekar writes that television sets were put in schools, and programmes on science and current affairs were specially produced for this purpose (Mankekar, 1999, p. 55). The emphasis on public education through television was also evident in the development of one strictly government controlled television station in India, which is called Doordarshan (DD). Doordarshan was the main television channel before India's opening of the market to foreign investment through economic liberalisation in the 1990s. For twenty years the government ran radio and television stations under one department together; it was not until 1997 that Doordarshan became a separate department (Mankekar, 1999, p. 55). A. Roy writes in his article on the development of popular culture and television India that the Indian government's only official television station Doordarshan had, from the beginning, has focused on a pedagogical formula of "government's achievement" and "national integration" (Roy, 2008, pp. 30-31). The use of only Hindi and English languages on Doordarshan indicates that national integration was only an ideal, as television in these languages were of no use to the majority of the Indians who lived in rural areas and did not speak those languages. This gap between broadcasting and viewing languages in India suggests one of the first reasons why local television might have a significant following in India.

In some ways the earliest television in India was almost like small community television; the audience were limited to a few cities, and the programmes were focused around a particular message, the nationalist ideal. However, this changed as within a short period of time Indian officials started to learn how they could make money from television advertisements. When Doordarshan first started showing commercials in 1976 the government authorities had no idea how much money could be generated. However, Doordarshan immediately began generating revenues and went from being completely financially dependent on government funding to a revenue generator for the Government of India within a decade. In 1976, when Doordarshan started advertising it earned $640,000; by 1987, the station was making approximately $130 million annually through the sale of advertisements (Singhal *et al.*, 1988, p. 226). As advertising income rose more money was invested into the government station's operating budget. Although other stations had begun to arise in India, this change in the economics of Indian broadcasting, an increase in commercialisation, established a very difficult media environment for small local television stations. Smaller stations would have found it difficult to compete with the powerful state-run television station that was generating millions of dollars from advertisements and spending similarly large amounts on their shows. Other problems that local television stations were facing included challenges purchasing both the hardware and software that were becoming necessary to produce and broadcast programmes.

During India's economic liberalisation in the 1990s there were tremendous changes in the nation's broadcasting, and smaller local stations soon faced competition from multi-million dollar foreign media corporations as well. The government channel received millions of dollars in advertisements from international brands such as Ponds and Colgate (Singhal *et al.,* 1988, p. 226). Indian channels had access to more international content, and some were now owned by international corporations. A controlling portion of STAR TV, for example, had been purchased by Rupert Murdoch. India also had to depend on other countries for broadcasting their television programmes through satellite systems. With satellite reception non-Indian owned television programmes were available more widely (McDowell, 1997, p. 151). The rise in transnational stations in India followed a similar pattern to the rise in television in general; Mankekar writes that in 1991, when the first transnational satellite programmes started broadcasting in India, only very affluent people were able to access the stations (Mankekar, 1999).

It is difficult to know how widespread television ownership in India was during this time; while Singhal *et al* claim that 52 per cent of rural and 88 per cent of urban Indian households had televisions in 1987, they note that their sample was skewed towards Hindi speaking households in the Delhi area (Singhal *et al.,* 1988, p. 226). My own experiences in more remote and non-Hindi speaking regions of India in the 1980s and 1990s lead me to believe the numbers were much lower in the rest of India. In Ladakh and similar areas of Jammu and Kashmir televisions were still relatively rare in the late 1980s, and certainly fewer than 50 per cent of households had televisions during this time period, even in the urban areas of these regions. The most recent Census of India data, which is some of the most reliable social data produced in India, puts 2011 national television ownership at 33.4 per cent in rural areas and 76.7 per cent in urban areas, and shows that television ownership has been generally on the rise in India during the past few decades, making it doubtful that the numbers would have been that high in the 1980s (Gov. of India, 2011).

In spite of these challenges the media environment in India for local television stations improved in some ways during the 1990s. Throughout India there was rapid construction of small local cable television distribution networks before any public policy for cable television was formulated, which allowed for further unregulated growth (McDowell, 1997, p. 161). The late development of television in India turned into an impressive growth during this time; while in the 1980s there were only 150 cable channels in India, in the early 1990s there were over 12,000 cable channels, and by the time of regulation in 1995 there were an estimated 100,000 (Sinclair, 2005). This rise in cable television channels in India signified the beginning of local television stations. Cable gave operators a fairly easy, and relatively inexpensive (compared to satellite) way of showing their own programmes. At the same time the cable method came with another set of problems for local television stations; they were not able to broadcast to large towns and cities because of the cost of running cables.

While the rise of cable channels is impressive, not all of these featured local or regionally specific content. Operators did not control the area that they could access; the cable channel distributors would allocate each cable operator a small area or population. Cable operators could then purchase the rights from the distributors to show programming from national and international channels, or show their own content. Thus, John Sinclair writes that just because a channel is called a "local channel" it does not always mean that it will broadcast any locally made or regionally specific programmes on its station (Sinclair, 2005). These were also short-lived media projects; during his research a decade later Sinclair found that many of the 1995 listed local channels were closed due to the costs of production, and some of those open only showed movies with crude advertising banners (Sinclair, 2005, p. 75). This broadcasting of other content on a local community television station is not specific to the Indian media context; for example, Doris Baltruschat notes in her article on the role of television and other technologies for traditional story telling among Canadian aboriginal communities, that the Aboriginal Peoples Television Network (APTN) in Canada purchases programming internationally, although Baltruschat notes that the network is still able to maintain a strong community focus (Baltruschat, 2004).

Even the existence of small community-focused television stations in rural India does not always mean that these stations empower rural people. P. Thomas writes in "The Ambivalent State and the Media in India: Between Elite Domination and the Public Interest" that the Indian government has problems enforcing their media policies because of the role of commercial ownership and the influence of political parties (Thomas, 2014). He argues that India's media management is defined both by a high level of control in the policies and a low level of actual regulation. Thomas analyses media ownership regulation by looking at the case study of the Sun TV network. The local television stations that arose on cable in India were soon influenced by corporations and politicians. Large corporations started buying small television stations and major political parties heavily invested into these television stations.

What does all of this tell us about how local media functions today in India? Some of the issues significant to local television stations in India are common to local stations around the world. The constant changes in media landscape have always been a challenge for the small local media broadcasters; whether using radio, television, or now high speed internet, the media method requires a great deal of financial resources and human involvement in order to fully function. The ups and downs of economic stability for local television are an ongoing battle. It is almost impossible for any small television station to function without a constant flow of funds. The impact of these issues on local television stations in India is that some depend upon larger media corporations.

Local television stations compete with large corporate-run television stations. They are constantly adopting new ways to survive, sometimes using their small size to their advantage as they can ideally design their programmes to meet the linguistic and religious needs of the viewers of a particular area. Yet this is not always effective, and most small stations do not survive because of lack of funding, or lack political/religious influence. As Higgins has discussed the ones that do survive are those that get most support from the community, thus using language or religion to mobilise community support may be important (Higgins, 1999).

One of the main reasons that people choose local media is that national and transnational media often ignores local or community events, unless it is something that requires national or global attention. Local events and community interests are rarely given equal attention. Roth provides the following typical example from 1983, when the First Peoples of Canada (now called First Nations of Canada) learned that government regulations required Canadian national television stations such as CBC and CANCOM (now Shaw Communications) to show programmes produced by local indigenous people (Roth, 2000). The existence of these regulations may make it seem like attention was being paid to community issues. However, the indigenous people soon learned that their programmes were broadcast in ways that made them inaccessible, such as being shown at 3:00 am in the early morning; by showing the programmes at unpopular hours the stations were fulfilling their legal obligations but did not actually support community growth (Roth, 2000, p. 257).

The Indian examples of local or community television show that there is no one model for this type of media. Higgins discusses community television as a mechanism that stays outside the corporate vision (Higgins, 1999, p. 640). Yet we can clearly see that many local television stations in India are a part of larger corporate structures. At the same time, as discussed earlier, he also claims that local media is meaningful as a process, and this is something that is possible to see in Indian examples. The types of successful language-based local television channels produced by members of the community, such those discussed in Chatterjee's work or that I observed in Kargil, can be thought of as classic local television stations or "community television" (Chatterjee, 2012). These are the similar to the type of media outlet that Higgins defines when he writes, "[t]he use of video by non-professionals for the purposes of personal and group empowerment, community communication and development, and social change came to be known as "community television" or "community video" (Higgins, 1999, p. 625). The one way that they differ, which may be significant, is that the Kargili station owners are media professionals; as will be discussed later in this book most of them reported working for national or international stations, and receiving a formal media education.

The First People's media that Roth discussed was founded in part to undermine the potential power of outside media within indigenous communities (Roth, 2000). Local television stations in India engage in similar processes when they resist conforming to majority cultural symbols through the use of programmes that feature minority languages and/or religious interest. Other aspects of community television, such as Hanusch's five features (discussed in more detail Chapter 2) are difficult to assess from a historical perspective, and require an in-depth study of particular community television settings in India (Hanusch, 2013).

The Kargil Region

The region of Ladakh is part of Jammu and Kashmir State of India, the northern-most state in the country. This region is divided into two districts, Leh and Kargil. According to the Census of India the population of Kargil district in the year 2011 was 119,307 (Gov. of India, 2011). The small population is spread on a large area of 5438.6 square miles (Centre, 2015). Kargil borders with Pakistan on its north-west edge, and this Himalayan town is situated at 8,780 feet above sea level. As anthropologist Jacqueline Fewkes writes:

> Ladakh is a region most often defined in relation to its surroundings. Perched on India's northern borders with

Pakistan and China, it is situated at the western edge of the Tibetan Plateau, between the Himalayas to the south and the Karakoram mountain range to the north (Fewkes, 2006, p. 20).

For six months of every year Ladakh is cut off with the rest of India during winter because of the cold and snow on the main highways that link Ladakh with rest of the world.

According to Fewkes, the Ladakh region obtained local communication facilities well before other rural regions in Himalayan Central and South Asia because of its importance in colonial politics and historical trade; the first post office in Ladakh was opened in 1875 and the first telegraph office was opened near Kargil in 1882 (Fewkes, 2009, pp. 85-86). Most of the communication facilities at this time were only available for colonial power and the wealthy traders. The first radio in Ladakh belonged to missionaries (Lone, 2013, p. 114). The major regional media started in 1971, when the Government of India opened Ladakh's first radio station for all those who could afford a radio (Morup, 2002, p. 7).

There is very little published about television specifically in Kargil. The Census of India, which is a detailed and extensive national census, is one of the vital sources of information about the role of media in the Kargil district. In 1871, the British colonial powers started the Census of India, and since then it has been regularly conducted once every ten years. The data from these surveys were once only available in specific government offices in hard copies, but are now available online for everyone. All of the data in the Census of India is by household, rather than collected from an individual person. Beside much other information about the households, one type of data that is collected is about household assets, whether or not the household own certain common items. These include a radio/transistor, a television, a computer/laptop, a telephone/mobile phone, a bicycle, a scooter/motorcycle/moped, and a car/jeep/van. The household asset data also includes the number of households that do not own any of these goods. This census is conducted in every part of

India and the data is available on district level. This breakdown of data helps me to look at Kargil district in comparison to other districts and also in comparison to state and national data. The information collected about the assets ownership shown in the charts from Census of India provides a great deal of information about the presence of media in Kargil today.

My main focus in using the Census of India is to look the number of television sets owned in Kargil; in addition I have looked at the number of households that are listed by the census of India as owning computers, telephones, and radios. The reason behind looking at all of these assets is that all these pieces of equipment are a part of the screen cultures, the different forms of media and their significance for users, in which Kargilis participate. Also, any one of these media technologies may be used to watch or listen to local television programmes.

From the 2011 Census of India data on the availability of televisions in Kargil district we can see that in the last ten years there has been a significant growth in television ownership in Kargil district. In 2001, there were 3,133; by 2011 that number jumped to 8,008 households for an over 25 per cent increase. This shows that there is definitely a growing interest in television in Kargil; however, we do not know why people are buying these televisions—which channels and shows they are interested in viewing. We also do not know if the purchase of the televisions between 2001 and 2011 was more for status or other reasons than for viewing purposes.

At the same time Kargil's television ownership numbers are still not very high. The 2011 census of India clearly demonstrates that Kargil is still ranked as the lowest in numbers of television ownership compared to other districts of Jammu and Kashmir State (Gov. of India, 2011). This may be because television was introduced in Kargil much later than in other parts of Jammu and Kashmir. Mankekar writes that Srinagar (the capital city in Kashmir) was one of the earliest cities to receive a television station; this was done by the government to counter alleged propaganda from neighbouring countries (Mankekar, 1999, p. 55).

In addition to television Kargil is also last in the state rankings in terms of telephone, radio, and computer ownership in all data from the 2011 Census of India. These are all related to the remote location and economic status of Kargil; the low numbers of these other assets show that the low numbers of televisions is not specific to televisions themselves but part of a larger trend of lower screen culture access. These assets also show significant growth. According to the Census of India in 2001, no households in the entire Kargil district owned a computer, however, by 2011 there were 1,005 computers in Kargil (Gov. of India, 2011).

Similar to the pattern with computers, the Census of India records a huge increase in telephone ownership in Kargili households in the period between 2001 and 2011. While there were only 897 households in Kargil with telephone sets in 2001, by 2011 that number had increased to 10,562 (Gov. of India, 2011). These numbers do not include the number of telephones used in government and military places as well. The Census of India data available for ownership of telephones does not specifically distinguish between types of phones that are being used in Kargil; while many may have smart phones that can access videos, a majority of these phones may be landlines or older cell phones that are only used for making calls. It is therefore hard to say how much the very high, 52.6 per cent, growth in telephone ownership has influenced Kargili screen culture (Gov. of India, 2011).

A very interesting trend in the graphs is the decrease in radio ownership in Kargil between 2001 and 2011. There is a steady decline in radio/transistor in Kargil in 2001 there were 11,340 and in 2011 there are fewer 10,895 sets (Govt. of India, 2011). The decrease was more in urban area 18.4 per cent as compare to rural areas 6.8 per cent (Govt. of India, 2011). This slow decrease of radio in rural areas was partly because of limited electricity supply in many villages of Kargil. This was the only asset tracked that declined in ownership in this decade, suggesting that there was a specific reason for its decline. Since many people in the Ladakh region have gotten their news from radios in the past this decline strongly suggests, although it does not prove, that other media sources are replacing radio as news sources.

Another interesting feature of the census data is that Kargil ranks third in the Jammu and Kashmir district comparisons for number of households that do not have any of the tracked assets. According to the 2011 Census of India, in 2001 29.8 per cent of households in Kargil did not have any of the listed assets, in 2011 that number shrank to only 19.4 per cent (Govt. of India, 2011). Many of the rankings of Kargil as last in ownership of specific assets could be due to its small population, as Kargil is one of the least populated districts in the state of Jammu and Kashmir. However, Kargil's ranking of third, rather than last, in overall asset ownership demonstrates that population size is not the only factor for assets ownership rankings.

If we compare percentages from the census shown in Figure 1, Figure 2 and Figure 3 below we can see that in 2011 a smaller percentage of households owned televisions in Kargil as compared to both state and national averages. In 2001 census data, 81.2 per cent of the households in Kargil reportedly did not own television sets, however by 2011 that number had lowered to only 56 per cent. In the state of Jammu and Kashmir the overall television ownership was much higher, 40.7 per cent in 2011, as compared to Kargil. This may be due in part to the history of television in the state, where, as discussed earlier, television was introduced much earlier than other parts of India to curb the growing popularity in Kashmir and Punjab of television programmes broadcast from Pakistan across the border (Mankekar, 1999, p. 55). The 25.2 per cent growth in television ownership in Kargil between 2001 and 2011 is a remarkably larger growth rate than the state and national (10.3 per cent and 15.6 per cent respectively) averages. These numbers suggest that the comparatively small number of households owning televisions in Kargil from 2001 to 2011 will change in the future if the increase in ownership remains at the same rate. Kargil's television ownership percentages in comparison to state and national ones may have already changed dramatically in the years since the last census.

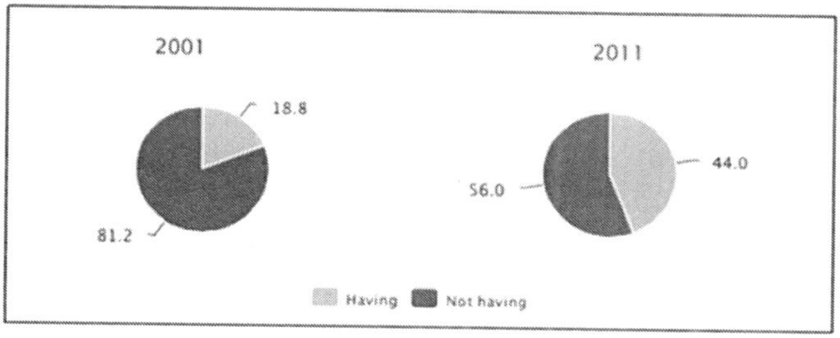

Figure 1: Percentage of households that own televisions in Kargil, Census of India (Govt. of India, 2011).

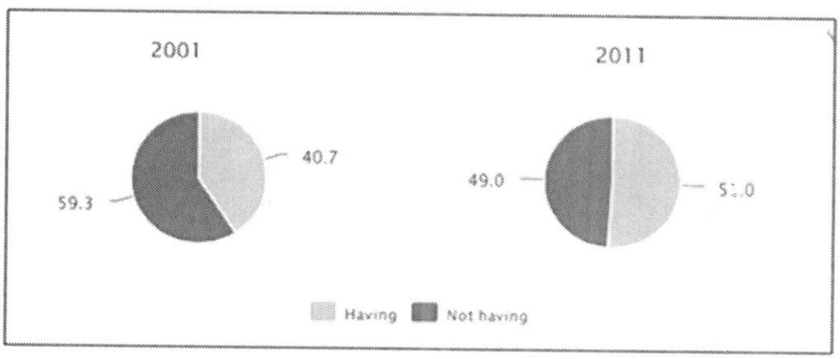

Figure 2: Percentage of households that own televisions in Jammu and Kashmir, Census of India (Govt. of India, 2011).

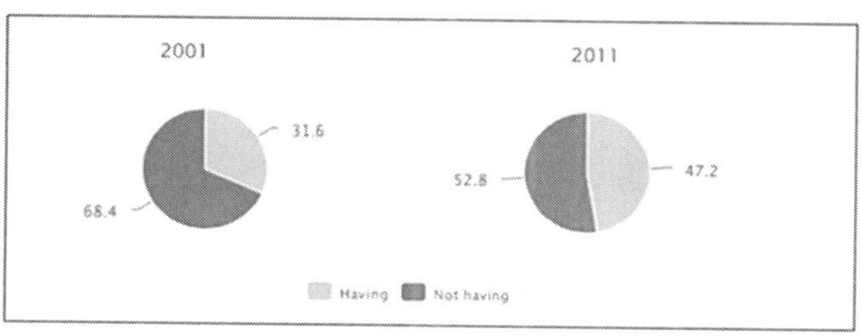

Figure 3: Percentage of households in India that own televisions, Census of India (Govt. of India, 2011).

It seems that television in particular is growing in Kargil; only television ownership numbers rose at a higher rate than the national growth numbers. For example, the growth of telephone shows a different pattern—the telephone ownership grew 52.6 per cent during 2001 and 2011, while in the state of Jammu and Kashmir ownership grew 62.7 per cent and all over India it was 54.1 per cent (Govt. of India, 2011).

The data collected during the census shows a significant social pattern in television ownership within the Kargil district as well. In rural areas 39 per cent of households have television, which is much lower than the national average. On the other hand 71.6 per cent of urban households own televisions, which is well above national averages (Govt. of India, 2011). Thus, the area in which the Kargili stations are operating and broadcasting has a significantly higher degree of access to television than the outlying areas of the region and those numbers are distinct from national patterns.

Overall the Census of India gives us an idea of how media access has improved in Kargil district in recent years, and that the rate of improvement has been very rapid. The remoteness of the region was not always an obstacle for new technologies to reach Kargil and people of Kargil are interested in adopting these new technologies quickly.

Chapter - 2

Background and Methods

As mentioned in the last chapter, my research focuses on the popularity of local media in Kargil. By asking if the success of local media in Kargil results from fulfilling the needs of the local community in ways that global media outlets cannot, I seek to better understand why this media is popular in the region, and what needs and/or desires it does actually meet for the local community. In order to explore these issues I first focus on the background literature that is relevant to this study, starting with what we know about the significance of local television based on communications literature today. I will then be examining existing literature on the role of language in Indian local television as many authors suggest that language is a major component of the popularity of local television stations in India. Globalisation and localisation are also important concepts to examine to understand the relationship between the global technologies and influences and these local stations. Finally, I will discuss the concept of media convergence, an issue that arose and gained significance during the course of my research.

The Significance of Local Television

In the article "Community Television and the Vision of Media Literacy, Social Action, and Empowerment" John W. Higgins, a media studies specialist, reviews the assumption that the American local media movement would create a media utopia where a variety of perspectives would be heard by viewers (Higgins, 1999). He uses critical communications theory to consider whether community television is actually empowering for local communities and critiques this utopian assumption; his methods include interviews with producers at independent stations and analysing the results. Higgins is concerned with the values of media literacy, a development of awareness of the self and others, and social change. He demonstrates that some of the purposes that community television serves may be universal. I agree with the author that media literacy is important and that community television stations all over the globe might have some similar purposes, as I found in Kargili local television station and Canada the First Peoples station. Higgins argues that the main factors that led to the establishment of community televisions in North America were a distrust of centralised social institutions and the common belief that average people had lost the rights to influence of the society (Higgins, 1999, p. 625). He writes that social change is mostly indirectly related to social media that does not cause immediate or direct social changes. According to Higgins, the most significant argument critiquing community television movements is that working for empowerment through community television does not take into account the structural changes necessary to address social inequities, but rather simply focuses on technology and "liberal pluralist dogma" (Higgins, 1999, p. 627). Higgins argues that the community media movement creates a space for the development and creation of a mechanism that stays outside the corporate vision (Higgins, 1999, p. 640). He concludes that local media is meaningful as a process, and therefore we must focus on its goals to be successful.

Other authors have written about the significance of local television for community identity and as a challenge to other media forms. Lorna Roth discusses Canadian First People's media in the article "Bypassing of Borders and Building of Bridges: Steps in the Construction of the Aboriginal Peoples Television Network in Canada" (Roth, 2000). In Canada, the

First Peoples started to recognise the potential of media to disintegrate their cultural power; at the same time they also recognised media as a mechanism for empowerment and development in their struggle to resist conforming to mainstream values, as well as a medium for resolving social tension and race relation issues (Roth, 2000, p. 255). The First People's media that Roth discusses was therefore founded, at least in part, to undermine the potential power of outside media within indigenous communities. Roth writes that in Canada the First Peoples started to recognise the potential power of outside media to disenfranchise their viewpoints and erode their cultural power (Roth, 2000). Community television is an answer to these outside influences; it is a tool for empowerment and resistance, as well as a medium for solving social and race relation problems (Roth, 2000, p. 255).

Many similar points come up in Folker Hanusch's article "Charting a Theoretical Framework for Examining Indigenous Journalism Culture" (Hanusch, 2013). Hanusch outlines five features of indigenous journalism culture, which can be related to the concept of local television as it is about community-based media. The five features include empowerment, "the ability to offer a counter-narrative", "language revitalisation [sic]", "reporting through a culturally appropriate framework", and fulfilling a "watchdog function" (Hanusch, 2013). Hanusch's five features are difficult to assess from a historical perspective, and require an in-depth study of particular community television settings, such as that in India.

In spite of popular journalisms' claims that the internet has "killed" niche television, recent studies suggest that local television stations such as public access channels remain a significant source of information for minority communities. In the article "Still Relevant? An Audience Analysis of Public and Government Access Channels" the authors Wenhong Chen, Marcus Funk, Joseph Straubhaar, and Jeremiah Spence, studied the use of public access channels in Austin, Texas (Chen *et al.,* 2013). They conducted a survey to analyse the audience for these channels, and found that they are important to underprivileged populations and minorities. They also noted that public access television has social capital for the viewers, that is to say that people who watch public access television were considered well informed by others. The authors suggest that the focus of literature on public, education, and government (PEG) channels has been centred on production instead of audience analysis, which creates problems in understanding these channels as a source of information for the public and also as an appropriate medium for public expression (Chen *et al.,* 2013).

Overall in the literature related to the significance of local television we can see that local or community based television can be significant to the communities that use them in a variety of ways; there is no simple checklist of features that make a local television station effective or successful. Later in the book I will address whether or not some of these patterns apply to local media in other parts of the world, particularly in India as the country of focus for this study.

Language in Indian Local Television

A common assumption in the literature on local television in India is that it is indigenously produced in the local language(s). While language plays a significant role in bolstering the viewership of local media in India, many of the language-focused channels are not what we would think of as indigenously produced. This is due, in part, to the types of language communities that exist in India. The size of linguistic communities varies considerably, however in a densely populated country like India local television viewers for a particular minority language channel can be in millions.

In the article "Globalisation and Grassroots: Local Cable Television Operators and their Household Subscribers in India" John Sinclair writes about how the different stages of cable television developed late in India, with a national system in 1982, but then grew quickly, from the 1980s

(150 cable channels) to the 1990s (12,000 cable channels) (Sinclair, 2005). He points out that at the same time of the rise of local language channels there was a debate in India about the presence of foreign channels in India (Sinclair, 2005). Sinclair's methods are based on literature reviews of published works, and interviews with cable suppliers and consumers; he employs empirical theory in his work, and emphasizes the value of understanding local and global as connected concepts. Sinclair argues that "tele-visual culture", which came after the opening of the market, did not over-run local culture, in spite of the fact that many have argued it as a "cultural invasion" (Sinclair, 2005). There is a considerable growth in regional language channels, but the competition for audience is absolutely won by the channels that show Indian film and film music, and are also able to indigenise the format of global commercial television and shows. Sinclair observes that several of India's "minority" and "regional" languages have tens of millions of speakers; for example there are 70 million Bengali speakers and 53 million Tamil speakers (Sinclair, 2005, p. 71). Furthermore these large language communities are diverse; even though physical boundaries between India and its neighbours are heavily guarded, languages such as Tamil, Urdu, and Bengali crisscross many borders. Thus, a linguistic minority may include people living in different countries, with different local interests.

Language-based local channels are also often funded by outsiders. As discussed in the last chapter, after economic liberalisation foreign investments started pouring in India (Singhal *et al.,* 1988). Some community members, politicians, and entrepreneurs realised that there was a huge market for the local television channels focusing on language. Once they established that community viewers liked watching programmes in their own language the trend started spreading in many other parts of India and local language-based channels became a successful broadcasting model. Now large media corporations in India like Zee TV broadcast in Hindi and

English on multiple channels, but also market channels with other South Asian languages, including Bengali, Urdu, Gujarati and Punjabi (Sinclair, 2005).

In spite of this, language-based channels do have significance in India as local television channels. Anshu Chatterjee discusses this issue in her article "Inequalities in the Public Sphere: Emergence of Community Television in India", where she writes about the value of community television in supporting India's diverse democracy (Chatterjee, 2012). In this article Chatterjee answers questions about how local television stations can survive in the competitive media world, and how community media functions in India today. Chatterjee's article is based on empirical research, using data from other publications, Indian ministries (such as the Ministry of Information and Broadcasting), and Indian media research groups, with case studies from the Punjab and Bengal regions of India. In her work she uses empirical theories of communication, and the discussion in this article is mainly descriptive rather than interpretive. Chatterjee points out that language in India is an identifying symbol that is used to form ethnic communities and leads to different forms of consumption (Chatterjee, 2012, p. 233). She comments that the term community applies specifically "to language-based ethnic groups" (Chatterjee, 2012, p. 230). She writes here about how ethnic community television channels have grown in India since the government opened its markets for foreign investment. There has been uneven growth of community television stations all over India, and the community television channels that have been most successful are not necessarily those from the wealthiest communities, but those that are supported by strong community organisations. Chatterjee writes that while "[t]he success of a competitive community media is linked to the strategic use of inter-institutional linkages at the community level", in contrast "the lack of such relationships undermines attempts by community enterprises to gain resources and form an audience base" (Chatterjee, 2012, p. 231). Chatterjee's work suggests that there is a form of "local media" recognisable throughout India; after my research it seems local media in India is more complex. In a diverse country such as India local media is worth studying as individual cases rather than as one whole; in Kargil the local media approach might be completely different than that of the local media in a small town in Punjab or Bengal.

In the book, *Screening Culture, Viewing Politics: An Ethnography of Television, Womanhood, and Nation in Postcolonial India* by Purnima Mankekar we see how language issues intersect with other issues in Indian television, such as nationalism and gender (Mankekar, 1999). This book is on research done in the 1990s by Mankekar. She writes about representations of gender and nationalism in shows that are broadcast on the Government of India owned and run television station Doordarshan. As discussed in the last chapter, Doordarshan has transformed from a medium for spreading government agendas to the nation into a commercial television station where, according to Mankekar, shows and programmes represent the powerful hegemonic class of Indian society (Mankekar, 1999). The author argues that the government television station that broadcasts programmes all over India creates television viewers into a hegemonic nation through shows about patriotism, family, sacrifice, and honour (Mankekar, 1999). National languages play a significant role in this process; Mankekar writes that there were allegations specifically in non-Hindi speaking states that the Government of India controls media languages. This was reflected in the breakdown of programmes shown during the prime time in 1985, when 46 per cent of the total programmes on Doordarshan were in Hindi, and 44 per cent of the programmes were in English (Mankekar, 1999, p. 61).

Globalisation and Localisation

The concept of globalisation, and its inverse—localisation—play an important role in this study. Globalisation has become a hotly contested phenomenon in many disciplines, as theorists from different disciplines have argued about the pros and cons of globalisation, as well as the ways in which it operates.

In the book, *Media and Cultural Studies*, editors Meenakshi Gigi Durham and Douglas M. Kellner have observed that for the critics of globalisation the term is simply a cover-up for more specific transnational forces, such as the strengthening of capitalism and imperialism in more areas of the world (Durham and Kellner, 2006). They also note that for supporters of globalisation it is a force of modernisation, progress, freedom, democracy, and an increase in wealth (Durham and Kellner, 2006).

Tony Schirato and Jen Webb write in the book, *Understanding Globalisation* that in the contemporary world globalisation is often defined as the power relations, practices, and technologies that have shape the modern world (Schirato and Webb, 2003). Schirato and Webb argue that many who are skeptical of globalisation see it as the continuation of European colonial expansion that was disturbed by the two world wars and the 'cold war'; for these authors globalisation is principally ideological present only in discourse than in reality. Schirato and Webb argue that if globalisation is really about equal excess and opportunities then why is the flow of research, development, science, and technology confined to selected sites and nodes of the capitalist network, especially in United States, Europe and Japan (Schirato and Webb, 2003). This, they claim, shows the limits of globalisation. These ideas of globalisation seem to apply to the Kargil case; they are reflected in the ways in which Kargili local stations have to depend on non-local technologies that are controlled by institutions in specific countries.

Globalisation is a combination of multiple complex layers of discourses, practices, values, and relations that have changed every aspect of human life. The complexity of these practices can be seen in the Kargil case. Twenty years ago it would have seemed completely impossible to run a local television station in a remote place like Kargil with no substantial financial investments. The power relations and practices that accompanied India's movement to open its market for foreign investment in the 1990s, and introduce cable in every corner of India as documented in the last chapter, made this possible. However, as the critics mentioned by Durham and Kellner above would point out, the possibilities of globalisation can mask power inequalities; Kargili local television stations are adopting newer technologies at a very fast speed but this does not mean that they have any control over these technologies.

Schirato and Webb argue that media industries produce a hegemonic medium, from corporations that are controlled by a handful of people and have unlimited power (Schirato and Webb, 2003). The owners of Kargili stations do not wield such power, and thus have to figure out different ways to send their programmes to viewers around the globe with little financial and political power. As will be discussed in later chapters, they localise the global technologies in a way that serves their purpose and at least temporarily levels the playing ground. But there is no surety about how long these solutions will last; Kargili local television stations are completely dependent on the big technology conglomerates that run the platforms that they use (as outlined in coming chapters). If companies such as Facebook and YouTube change their policies then the local stations will not have any access to the international viewers. International media technologies that belong to a few selected countries are not the only powerful players in this media situation; as mentioned by one Kargili journalist in an interview the stations are also completely dependent on national institutions such as the cable operators and internet providers.

The dependence of local media on larger entities that can control media access is common in many parts of the world. In an anthropological study of global online communities Samuel Wilson and Leighton Peterson observe,

> Although there have been examples of effective use of the Internet by small groups-such as the Zapatista movement's successful use of the Internet to gain support for their cause (http://www.ezln.org) or the survival of Belgrade's web-based Radio B92 in the late 1990s (http://www.b92.net) in many countries there have been intensive state efforts (of widely varying effectiveness) to regulate and control Internet based access to information (Wilson and Peterson, 2002, p. 452).

While media localisation is therefore possible—seemingly made possible by global technologies—it can also be blocked by the same. This is why Wilson and Peterson review a number of works that call for "continuing analyses of power relations, global capital, and the role of subaltern/minority peoples in the emergence of new media processes and products" (Wilson and Peterson, 2002, p. 455).

One popular way of discussing the media and globalisation that highlights the relationship between global and local media is through the use of Arjun Appadurai's idea of the "mediascape", which is a type of globalisation that addresses not only the technologies of media that are globally shared, but also "the images of the world created by these media" (Appadurai, 1990, p. 9). Appadurai developed the idea of "scapes", different sites for globalisation, in his book, *Disjuncture and Difference in the Global Cultural Economy*. According to Appadurai, the mediascape tends, "to be image-centred, narrative-based accounts of strips of reality" (Appadurai, 1990, p. 299).

In the article, "Embedded Aesthetics: Creating a Discursive Space for Indigenous Media", Faye Ginsburg uses Appadurai's ideas about globalisation to write about a situation similar to the Kargili local stations that I studied; she examines the role of indigenous media in Australia. Ginsburg writes,

> Appadurai argues for situated analyses that take account of the interdependence of media practices with the local, national, and transnational circumstances that surround

> them (Appadurai 1990:7). Using such a model for indigenous media helps to establish a more generative discursive space for this work which breaks what one might call the fetishizing of the local, without losing a sense of the specific situatedness [sic] of any production (Ginsburg, 1994, p. 366).

This means that the mediascape idea helps us to understand local media as part of a larger dialogue with the forces of globalisation, rather than as special exceptions to globalisation, while still emphasising the ways in which local media is not just a global product, but specific to the place that produced it.

Robert W. McChesney writes in the article "Global Media, Neoliberalism, and Imperialism" that globalisation is more appropriately called neoliberalism, as its goal is business domination both nationally and internationally. McChesney argues that much like the oil and automotive industries, the media and entertainment industries are also becoming a global oligopoly. He claims that the expansion of a global media system is not only limited to economic implications, but that it has significant cultural and political implications as well, especially with regard to political democracy and imperialism (McChesney, 2001, p. 12). McChesney writes that the current era is commonly known as one of globalisation, a technological revolution, and democratisation, and that in all of these three fields media and communication play the defining role (McChesney, 2001). If this is true then the most defining aspects of our time period are located in media, and the questions that we ask about the media are very important. McChesney argues that common idea of globalisation as a natural force that spreads capitalism is misleading; the globalisation of economy and culture would be impossible without a commercial media system that deliberately promotes it on a global level (McChesney, 2001). In this book I would like to consider how the local role of Kargili television stations, and their links to global media, fit into this argument.

Media Convergence

Another significant body of literature on a concept relevant to the purposes of this study is that of media convergence. In the article, "Convergence Culture: Where Old and New Media Collide", Henry Jenkins describes media convergence as a combination of multiple media activities, and the movement of contents on different media platforms (H. Jenkins, 2006). In the book chapter, "Flow and Mobile Media Broadcast Fixity to Digital Fluidity", Kathleen Oswald and Jeremy Packer write that today's age the media is defined by these different platforms; media success is no longer about keeping a viewer on one transmission, now viewers are being kept busy through multiple screens at different times and in different spaces. All these screens—televisions, computers, tablets, mobile phones—work in concert to connect consumers to their information (Oswald and Packer, 2011). In the book, *The Wireless Spectrum: The Politics, Practices, and Poetics of Mobile Media,* editors Kim Sawchuk, Barbara Crow and Michael Longford write in the introduction that users should know that mobile and portable technologies are a component of a bigger network made up of all the inter-operable devices that can relay groups of information from one place to another; a cell phone is no longer just a mobile device for talking but becomes a tool for all-round transformation of social practices (Sawchuk, Crow, and Longford, 2010). Similarly Jenkins observes that media convergence involves numerous media companies cooperating with each other, and media consumers, who are moving between different media platforms to find the content they want (H. Jenkins, 2006).

For these reasons Jenkins argues that media convergence should not be seen as just a technological process that is responsible for bringing together different media functions into the same device (H. Jenkins, 2006). The consumer plays a very important role in circulation of the media contents from different media systems, and therefore how media crosses between different national borders. Convergence should be looked at as a shift in culture, in which consumers are inspired to find out new information and to make connections with diverse forms of media content that is continuously changing (H. Jenkins, 2006). This concept will be particularly significant later in Chapter 4, in which I discuss the adoption of new communications technologies—in this case a smart phone app—that are used by the Kargili stations to increase access to local television news programmes in unique new ways.

Methods

There are a number of different methods that I have used in this study to better understand the role of local media in Kargil. These include interviews, media content analysis, a survey, and text analysis.

I conducted interviews with the owners of local television stations, as well as employees who work at the stations. The interview questions, as shown in Figure 4 below, focus on a variety of topics of interest, including the programming, language, advertisements, funding, role of the television stations, viewers, coverage, growth, and reaching programmes beyond local communities. I used multiple sources for my interview research, including the owners of the local television station, people who work for those stations—both journalists and programme editors—and some Kargili television viewers. The individual questions asked from the list in Figure 4 vary depending on the person interviewed. The goal of conducting these interviews was to gather primary data on my topic, to find out from the source about the circumstances through which the first local television stations were developed. The interviews were also intended to help me to understand the communities associated with these sites, and gather individual stories about the impact of this regional media in Kargil. Their answers have been provided in this book; some answers are provided anonymously to protect the privacy of individuals when necessary, and some non-essential but indentifying information may also have been changed for this reason.

The Role of Local Media in Ladakh (India)

1. Who started this station?
2. When was the station started?
3. Were you involved with its development?
   (a) [If YES on #3] Why did you start this station?
   (b) [If YES on #3] How did you gain knowledge about running a (type of media- television or radio) station?
4. What kind of programming is on this station?
5. In what language is most of the programming?
6. Do you have advertisements on the channel?
7. Do you receive funding for the station?
8. What are the sources of funding for the station?
9. What do you think is the role this station plays in the community?
10. Who views this station?
11. How many viewers do you have, on average?
12. How much area does the station coverage reach?
13. How do you think your station differs from other television stations that viewers might watch?
14. Has the growth of the internet impacted your station at all?

Basic Demographic Questions

Note: This information is collected for general analysis purposes only, to observe larger social patterns, and will not be associated in publication with the answers provided by identifiable individuals.

1. Are you male or female?
2. Where do you live?
3. Where were you born?
4. When were you born?
5. What religion are you?
6. What is the highest level of education you have finished: (a) none, (b) up to 5th class, (c) 8th class, (d) 10th class, (e) 12th class, (f) college, or (g) graduate school.

Figure 4: Interview Questions.

The second method used in this study was content analysis. I conducted a detailed content analysis of the programmes that are broadcast from three local television stations that were currently broadcasting programmes in Kargil district. The programmes that I analysed were those that were available for viewing online through video sharing websites such as YouTube, station websites, social networks, and online news websites. These programmes included news, documentaries, entertainment, current affairs, and advertisements. The types of information collected are listed below in Figure 5.

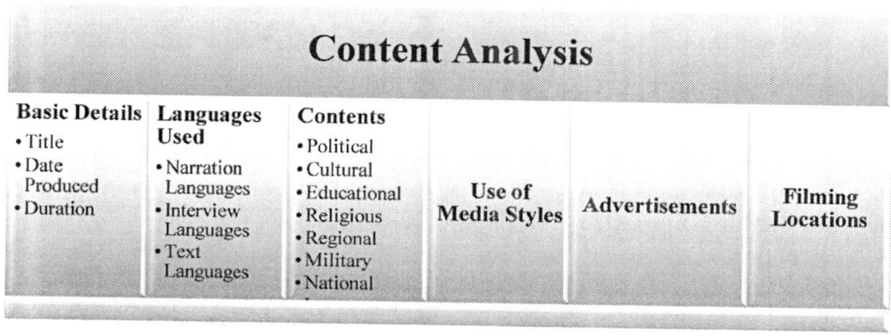

Figure 5: A list of the types of information collected for the television programme content analysis.

The information collected from the content analysis work was used to study and learn more about the types of programme that are broadcast in Kargil. All of the information collected through this method helps me to better understand how the standards for local Kargili television stations compare to those of other national and international stations. I also looked at the similarities and differences in the programme contents of each station. This is important because if the contents are somewhat similar we can not only ask why they are similar, but also why a small place like Kargil would need a number of local television stations.

The third method that I used to conduct this research was to collect data from television viewers using an online survey for people living in different parts of India. I conducted this survey completely online using SurveyMonkey, which is a web-based survey company used by many individuals and academic institutions (SurveyMonkey, 2015). The purpose of this research study is to understand the role that local television and other media outlets have in India; in the survey I tried to find out more viewers of these television stations. I designed the questions to learn more about the general public's perception about local media, and to investigate if the local media has a similar impact on different communities. This survey includes a set of sixteen questions arranged in three sections—viewing, local television, and demographics—as shown in Figure 6 below.

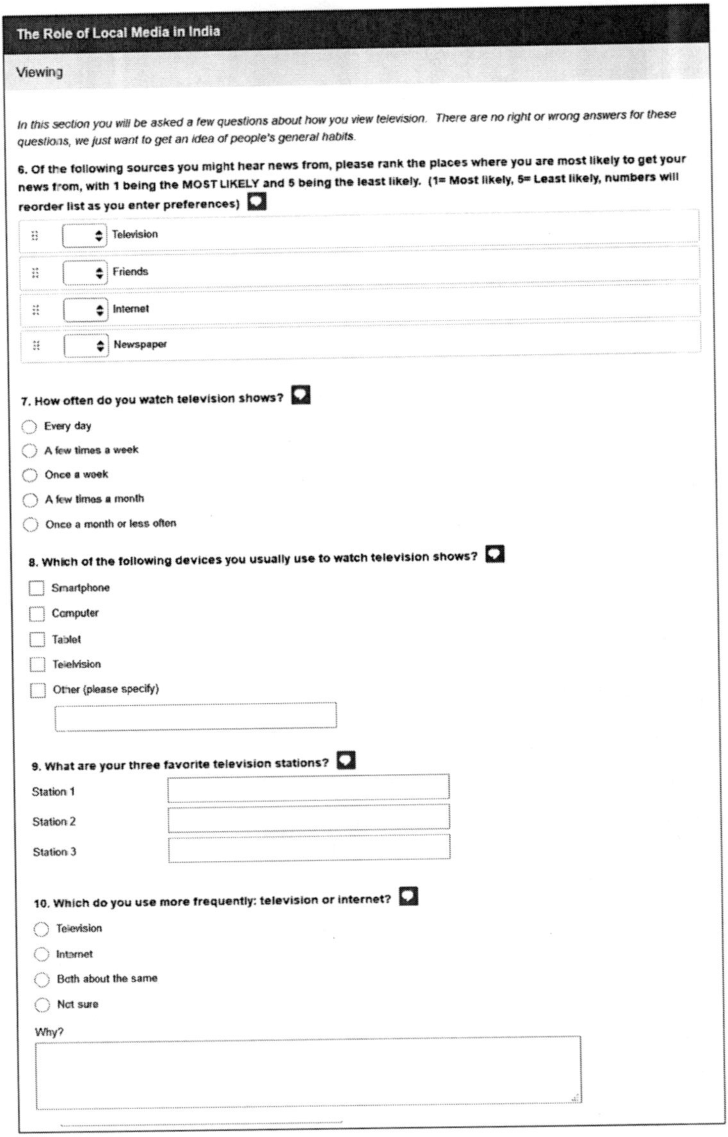

The Role of Local Media in India

Viewing

In this section you will be asked a few questions about how you view television. There are no right or wrong answers for these questions, we just want to get an idea of people's general habits.

6. Of the following sources you might hear news from, please rank the places where you are most likely to get your news from, with 1 being the MOST LIKELY and 5 being the least likely. (1= Most likely, 5= Least likely, numbers will reorder list as you enter preferences)

- Television
- Friends
- Internet
- Newspaper

7. How often do you watch television shows?

- Every day
- A few times a week
- Once a week
- A few times a month
- Once a month or less often

8. Which of the following devices you usually use to watch television shows?

- Smartphone
- Computer
- Tablet
- Television
- Other (please specify)

9. What are your three favorite television stations?

Station 1

Station 2

Station 3

10. Which do you use more frequently: television or internet?

- Television
- Internet
- Both about the same
- Not sure

Why?

11. In what language(s) do you listen to television programs? (click all that apply)

- ☐ Punjabi
- ☐ Marathi
- ☐ Telegu
- ☐ Kashmiri
- ☐ Tamil
- ☐ Urdu
- ☐ Kannada
- ☐ Hindi
- ☐ Bengali
- ☐ Malayalam
- ☐ English
- ☐ Gujrati
- ☐ Ladakhi
- ☐ Other (please specify)

The Role of Local Media in India

Local Television

The questions on this page are about local television; by local television we mean the stations that are broadcast specifically within your community and cover topics specifically of interest to your community.

12. What are the names of three local television stations in your area?

Station 1:

Station 2:

Station 3:

13. Do you think your region needs more local television stations or fewer?

- ○ More
- ○ Fewer

Why?

14. Do you think local television stations are important?

- ○ Yes
- ○ No
- ○ Not sure

Why?

15. What kinds of programs should local television broadcast?

Figure 6: Content sections 1 and 2 of the online survey.

The information collected from the survey was used to analysis and study the role that local television and other media outlets have in Kargil, and throughout India. This provides not only a detailed view of Kargil, but also a comparative view of the role of local media.

During my research I was surprised to find that Kargili local television stations have adopted and transformed a type of social media for their own purposes. WhatsApp is a mobile messaging app that can be used on smart phones, computers, and other devices, and allows users to exchange messages that include text, video, images, links, and user comments.

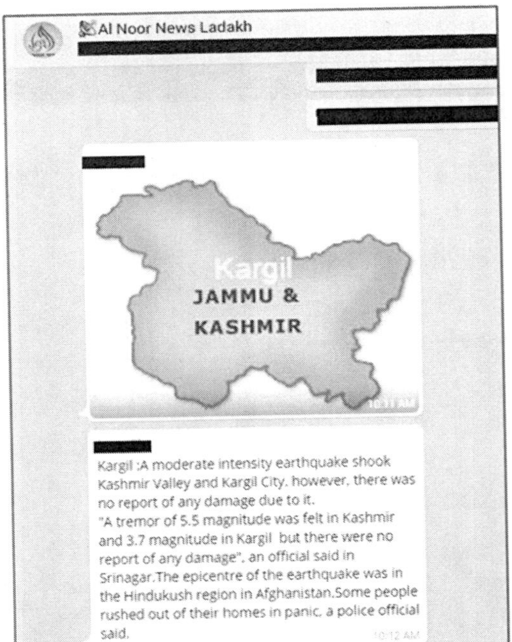

Figure 7: A screen shot from Kargil Today station's WhatsApp group page.

The use of WhatsApp was an unexpected component of my work, but quickly became important for understanding the role of local stations in Kargil. I found that all three of the major local stations in Kargil use WhatsApp to communicate news, as shown below in Figure 7.

After becoming a member of these local television stations' WhatsApp groups I was able to participate and observe the groups, doing a digital ethnography. I was a member of these stations for many months and closely monitored the content sharing of information in these groups to understand how these groups function as media outlets. To analyse the use of WhatsApp I performed content analysis, looking at the kinds of information shared, as well as how often information and news appears in these groups. I have also paid attention to the role of administrator of the group, and how group members participate in discussions and contribute to the information shared in these groups. I have used multiple examples from the WhatsApp groups later in this book to trace how live news develops into a full story in this new media format.

In this book I bring together these different methods and the various sources of information to explore from a holistic perspective how Kargil's local television stations play a significant role in the region.

The Local Stations of Kargil

During the course of my research I focused on studying three local stations: Kargil Today, Al Noor News Ladakh, and S TV Ladakh. These were not the only local stations in Kargil; there were also two other stations in Kargil that are run by religious organisations. The latter two stations were, however, special interest media outlets rather than classic local media; all the contents from the two religious organisations were either religious or related to the organisations. For this reason I did not include these two stations in my analysis. My research also did not cover all news media in the area as I am not addressing the role of the government run radio station, government television station, and small local print media in Kargil.

The first station I studied is Al Noor News Ladakh. Al Noor is translates as "The Light". According to the owner Al

Noor News Ladakh—also called Al Noor News Network—was started in March 5, 2009 and was the first private news broadcasting channel of Ladakh. According to the station owner, the news network was started with an intention to provide "infotainment" and also to function as media awareness forum for the people of Kargil. Al Noor produces and telecasts news, talk shows, advertisements, and documentaries. Their programmes are produced in multiple languages, including Urdu, Hindi, Purig, and Shina. Reportedly around 30,000 viewers watch Al Noor programmes on television sets in Kargil. Some of the programmes are also available on the internet through apps, social networks and YouTube (Noor Ul Islam, 2015b). The owner of Al Noor, who was born in Kargil, has a degree in Mass Communication, Advertising & Journalism which he received from a university outside of Ladakh (Noor Ul Islam, 2015b). The network is an independent broadcaster through "the Cable Television Networks (Regulation) Act 1995 ACT NO. 7 OF 1995 by Studio 360 Media Corporation" and all parts of the station are headquartered in Kargil (Al Noor News Ladakh, 2015b).

The second Kargili television station is Kargil Today. According to the owner of the station—who is also its editor-in-chief—the television station was started on December 31, 2012. Kargil Today station is located completely in Kargil and telecasts programmes from there. Kargil Today produces and telecast news, talk shows, advertisements, and documentaries on subjects such as education, politics, health, and sanitation. Their programmes are produced in Urdu, Hindi, English, and Purig. In interview the station's editor-in-chief estimated that around 20,000 viewers watch Kargil Today programmes on television sets in Kargil, and more than 100,000 people are watching the station through the internet (Khalo, 2015). A large number of internet viewers are Kargili students who go out of town for an education. Some of Kargil Today's programmes are also available through mobile phone apps, social networks and YouTube (Khalo, 2015). The owner has a degree in mass communication, with a major in journalism and advertisement from a university outside of Ladakh, and has also received training in editing, photography, and videography outside Ladakh (Khalo, 2015).

The final station featured in this research is S TV Ladakh. According to the owner and director of S TV Ladakh, this new station was started in 2014. S TV is located completely in Kargil as well, and telecasts programmes from there. S TV produces and telecasts news, current affairs, and advertisements. A majority of the programmes on S TV are done in Hindi and Urdu but the station has recently started using the Ladakhi, Balti, Purig and Shina languages too. The owner/director reports that around 10,000 people watch the S TV shows through cable in Kargil (N. Hussain, 2015). Some of the stations' shows are available on YouTube and S TV also sends its news through mobile app WhatsApp (N. Hussain, 2015). The owner has many years of experience in camera work and editing; he has worked for the state run television station Doordarshan (N. Hussain, 2015).

Chapter - 3

Programme Content and Text Analysis

As part of the research for this book I did a detailed content analysis of 87 programmes out of the hundreds that are produced by the local television stations that are currently telecasting programmes in Kargil district. The programs that I analysed are all those that were available online on social media and video sharing websites, posted between January 2011 and March 2015. The analysed programmes come from three local stations: Kargil Today, Al Noor News Ladakh, and S TV Ladakh.

While each of these three local stations that I analysed has their own role to play in Kargil's media, they share some common features. The owners and producers of these three stations have formal education in media, are working with national and international news organisations, and have extensive experience in the field. Each of them has therefore brought their training and expertise from other media venues to shape the Kargili local stations.

Once the programmes from these stations were limited in viewership to a small part of Kargil on televisions alone, however that has changed in recent years. The Kargil stations have benefited from media convergence as social media, video sharing websites and apps have made these programmes available to watch in any part of the world on a variety of devices such as computers, tablets, and cell phones. Kargil Today's programmes have been available on YouTube since January 2011; their programmes before February 2013 were under the name of "Hosain Ibn Khalo Network (Pvt) Ltd. Voice of Kargil". Al Noor News Ladakh programmes have been available online since July 2012. The third station, S TV Ladakh, is started later and their programmes have been available since December 2014. While S TV Ladakh has only a few programmes posted on YouTube, it now—like the other two stations—sends a significant amount of news and information on the cell phone messaging app "WhatsApp", a phenomenon that I will discuss later in my next chapter. Programmes from these three stations are commonly reposted on video sharing websites and social media by viewers as well.

The presence of Kargili local stations on YouTube has some clear patterns. While the number of programmes from these stations posted online was at first growing it has been decreasing more recently. In 2011, there was only one program posted on YouTube, and in 2012 there were only three programmes from the stations available online; all of these were only from Kargil Today and Al Noor News Ladakh. In 2013 these two stations increased their online presence, and 41 new programmes were posted on YouTube. In 2014, S TV Ladakh also started posting some of its programmes on YouTube. Even after the addition of one more station, however, the total number of programmes posted on YouTube in 2014 dropped to only 36. I attribute this drop to a change in the types of media technologies these stations are using; as I will discuss in the next chapter this is perhaps because of the increased use of mobile applications such as WhatsApp instead of more traditional computer-based media such as YouTube. The lower number of Kargili stations' programmes appearing on YouTube continued in early 2015; in the first four months of 2015 there were only six programmes were posted by these three stations.

The Programmes on YouTube

The average length of the viewed Kargili stations' episodes varies between the stations. S TV Ladakh's are the shortest, with the average programme timing at 3:56 minutes. Kargil Today's average posted programme length is 8:03 minutes, while Al Noor News Ladakh has an average of 10:18 minutes. The average length of episodes for these television stations also increases from 2:73 minutes in 2011 to 12:20 minutes in 2014.

Looking at these stations' four most watched programmes on YouTube can give a good sense of the types of programmes that are offered here, and the general contents of these programmes.

The first programme I will discuss, "*Kareena & Saif Kargil Visit, By Hosain Ibn Khalo*", is one of the earliest shows produced by Kargil Today. This is a 2:44 minute short news video about some Bollywood stars visit to Kargil. The titles are basic text, written all in English. In this video clip the station shows a large crowd of fans standing around the hotel where the movie stars are staying. A song from a local album is playing as background music. The owner of the hotel is shown talking about the difficulties of running a hotel in a remote place like Kargil, and the video ends again with basic titles. This video was viewed 2640 times on YouTube.

The second most viewed Kargili stations' programme on YouTube was also produced by Kargil Today. This programme, viewed 2124 times, is called "*Latest Kargil Today News Headlines 21-02-2013 .mpg*". This is a 7:25 minutes news headline show. The graphics are similar to those found on national and international news outlets. The titles are in English only. In this show Kargil Today's logo appears on the screen. The news is read in Urdu by anchors, and all of the news items read are local or related to the Kargil area. There are advertisements for local businesses in English, Urdu, and in local languages.

Another programme produced by Kargil Today, the third most viewed programme on YouTube, is titled "*KT Face to*

Face Talk with Sonam Wangchuk SECMOL Ladakh Part 1". This is presented as a talk show with a man who runs an organisation in the region. It is a long talk show divided into two parts on YouTube; the first part is 25:59 minutes, and the second part is 18:49 minutes. The first part of this programme was viewed 1849 times however the second part is viewed only 406 times.

The fourth most viewed show from the Kargili stations is titled "*Annual Ceremony of Reach Ladakh*"; it is a 2:06 minutes show produced by Al Noor News Ladakh in January 2014. This show highlights an event; a local internet news site's annual ceremony. Both still and video images are used in the show, without any narration. The titles are in English and the station logo is in Urdu.

The types of programmes and topics are also increasing from just basic videos to well structured news with reporters in different parts of the region. Some programmes are called "live telecast". There are telephone interviews with people who live in different parts of India, as well as videos that were shot in other parts of India; all these events have direct links to Kargilis either by political, social, religious, cultural, and other ties.

The Viewers on YouTube

The number of viewers of these programmes on YouTube fluctuates greatly between 2011 and 2015. In 2011, the only video posted was viewed 2640 times; in 2012 there were three posted shows but only 768 viewers. The big difference in viewers between 2011 and 2012 is that the earlier one features Bollywood stars, thus there is a greater possibility that viewers out of Kargil might have been interested in watching the video. The 41 episodes in 2013 had a clear increase in viewers, with a total of 11149 viewers; however, since then the Kargili stations' viewership on YouTube has been continuously decreasing. Looking at the average number of views per month sorted by year in Figure 9 below helps to see the significance of this pattern of posting shows on YouTube.

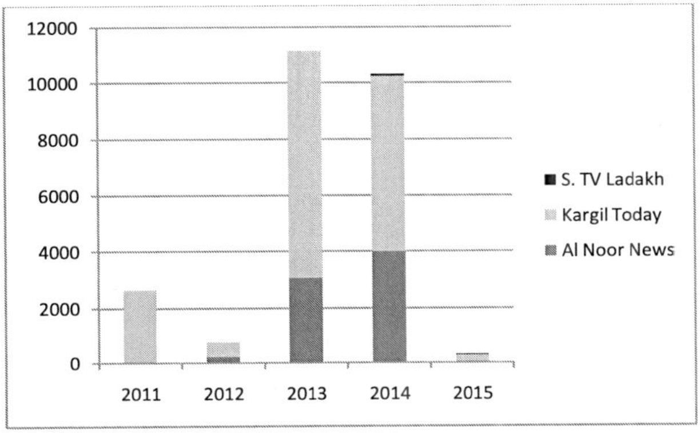

Figure 8: Total number of YouTube viewers for the three stations during the online time period 2011-2015.

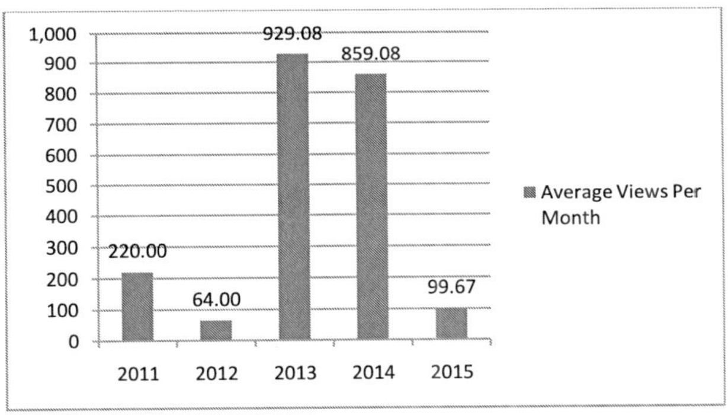

Figure 9: Average number of views per month, by year. This average allows us to compare the partial data from 2015 with whole years in the previous years.

The average number of views per month in 2011 is much higher than 2012 and 2015 even though there was only one programme uploaded on YouTube in 2011. In last five years—the date when programmes started appearing on YouTube—2013 has the highest number of viewers per month. In 2014, the number went down, and in the portion of 2015 analysed the numbers of views are much lower. The decrease in numbers of programmes appearing on video sharing sites, and the number of viewers, is most likely because of the role of technologies in the region. The poor internet connection in Kargil makes it difficult to participate in video sharing and other online forums; one of the correspondents from Kargil Today told me in an interview that the internet in Kargil is unreliable, sometimes for days there is no internet connection (Khalo, 2015). The station owners are adopting newer communications technologies that are reliable, cheaper, and faster, which I will discuss later in the next chapter.

Similar patterns of change are also reflected in the viewer's comments; 2013 has the highest number of viewer comments followed by 2014, which still has much lower numbers of comments than the previous year. One surprising thing about the YouTube presence of these videos is that while there does seem to be a dedicated viewership, the audience participation in YouTube is very small. Although all of the programmes are open for comments on average there is only one comment per programme in most years, and 1.85 comments per programme in 2013. The online forum for Kargili television stations is not a fully participatory screen culture.

Categorising the Programmes

When performing content analysis on these programmes from Kargili television stations I was interested in better understanding what types of programmes were offered. Assuming that the stations consider the programmes uploaded to YouTube significant, these should give an accurate representation of the main media priorities of local television stations in Kargil. In order to perform content analysis I divided the programmes into five categories: news, documentaries, entertainment, current affairs, and advertisements. To ensure that I classified programmes into categories empirically I designed a set of criteria, included below, to guide my analysis. While some programmes may have fit multiple categories I tried to employ these definitions strictly to determine into which category the programme best fit. My category criteria were written as followed before I started my analysis:

- News shows are those that present new information about recent events; they claim to be factual.

- Documentaries are nonfiction works that give information about a topic, for a particular purpose. They may be for educational purposes, used to argue a point of view, or intended to explore a question. This excludes pieces that are primarily focused on discussion of ideas about events, which fall under "Current affairs".
- Entertainment can be any type of show that is meant primarily to entertain others; no educational content or information is given.
- Current affairs are pieces that are made primarily to discuss ideas about important events, with viewpoints of the television producers and/or their viewers. They are similar to documentaries in that they may argue a point of view or explore a question, but are different because their focus is on different views about events.
- Advertisements are shows that are intended only to sell something, either a programme or product to viewers.

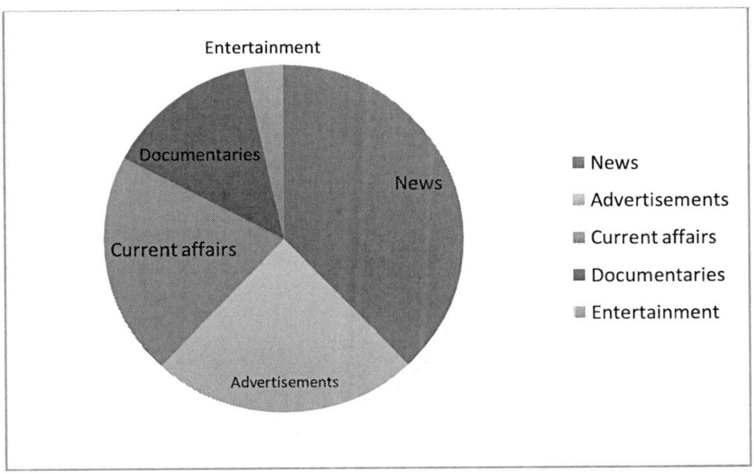

Figure 10: Percentages of different categories of shows selected and posted for showing on YouTube, in order of most to least number of episodes in category.

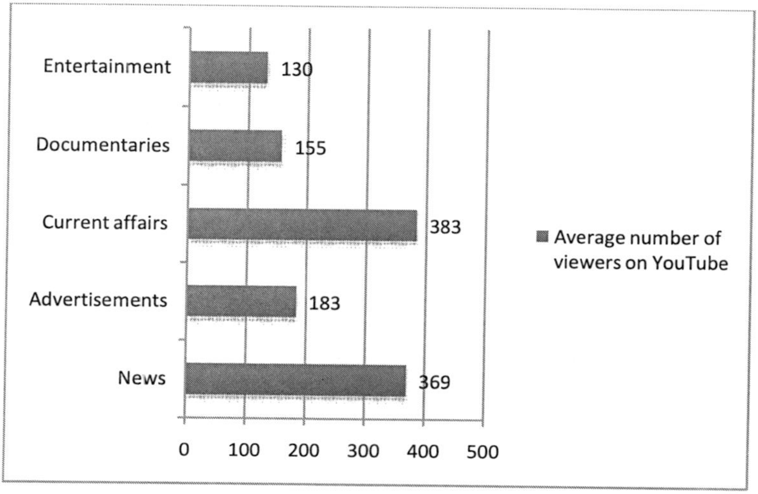

Figure 11: Average number of viewers for an episode on YouTube, arranged by episode category.

When classified the results of this content analysis were as shown in Figure 10 and Figure 11.

News is both the most posted and most watched type of programme on YouTube from these three television stations. The news programmes are 33 per cent of the posted shows; news and current affairs, categories that overlap considerably, are together 54 per cent of the programmes offered. From all the shows that are posted on YouTube news and current affairs are the most watched online. This pattern in the programme types was reflected in the interview with the editor-in-chief of Kargil Today, who said that a large segment of Kargilis—including the elderly and students who are studying outside Kargil—miss the news about Kargil, and that is why he started Kargil Today as a community-based station; the station was originally conceived as a media outlet where people get the news and information (Editor, Kargil Today, 2015).

As shown in the examples of popular episodes discussed earlier in this chapter, a majority of the YouTube posted programmes from these stations that are news are about local events and issues. News stories produced by all these stations are very similar in content. The news are telecast in different forms such as headlines, a complete summary of events with news readers and reporters in the field, or sometimes only an un-narrated video recording of the function with titles in English and/or Urdu. A majority of the news presented in these shows focuses on the local, however sometimes national and international news are included, for example, there was a New Year's special from Kargil Today in which an overview of national and international news from the year were presented in English.

The current affairs programmes on Kargil Today and Al Noor often feature interviews with important people from or within the region. These are shown as very long talk shows, and—as the category is based on the idea of presenting different views—these shows always contain dialogue between different people. One example of this type of programme is shown in the screen shot in Figure 12 below, a current affairs programme in which an Al Noor News Ladakh anchor is talking with a Ladakhi politician. This interview was conducted just before the national elections. During the election period

Figure 12: Screenshot from Face to Face Talk with Thupten Tsewang Al Noor News Ladakh, 2015 (Al Noor News Ladakh, 2014a).

all the politicians, different party candidates representing the region, gave interviews to these local television stations. While current affairs programmes are therefore an important political tool the category is not just limited to political topics only; other current affairs episodes feature important persons such as local activists and sports personalities.

Kargil Today and Al Noor News Ladakh have both also produced a number of short documentaries that focus on local issues. One such example is a documentary produced by Al Noor News Ladakh in 2015. The title of the programme is called "*Aawam ke Aawaz (Voice of the People) Sharchey Village boycott coming assembly elections, due to Lack of basic needs! Like Road Connectivity, Electricity & School*" (Al Noor News Ladakh, 2015).

Figure 13: Screenshot from "Aawam Ke Aawaz" documentary from Al Noor News Ladakh, 2015 (Al Noor News Ladakh, 2015a).

This is a documentary about a unique approach taken by the inhabitants of a remote village in Kargil district to show their anger towards the politicians and authorities. The story here focuses around the main problem of the village, that there is no motorable road link between the village and other places. The programme explains that the nearest road to the village is three miles away, and people carry their goods on animals or on their backs through a tough mountainous rocky path. The whole documentary is set in the Sharchey village. In Figure 13 a screenshot taken from the documentary shows that the villagers have no road for vehicles; even today goods are bought on animals and people have to walk miles.

Some of the stories in these documentaries focus on the role of Indian Army in Kargil. As Kargil is a border district, on the contended border with Pakistan, there is a huge presence of the Indian Army in the area. In interview the editor-in-chief of Kargil Today noted that since the 1999 Kargil War the army has been helping locals, opening schools, and facilities for the handicapped. The army invites local media to cover their functions and events (Editor, Kargil Today, 2015). One documentary that focuses on this role of the army in Kargil is called "*Umeed Ki Kirn (Ray of Hope)*" (Al Noor News Ladakh, 2015).

Figure 14: Screenshot from "Umeed Ki Kirn" documentary on Al Noor News Ladakh, 2013 (Al Noor News Ladakh, 2013).

This is a story about a girl getting eye surgery; in the documentary family members mention that they would not have been able to afford the surgery without the help of the Army. This is a personal interest documentary with emotional scenes, such as that in Figure 14 a screenshot from the documentary that shows the girl, after the success of her eye surgery, being presented a gift by the military during a function specially organised by the military to celebrate the occasion. The Indian army always invites local media to cover these types of functions.

Advertisement videos are the second biggest category posted on YouTube but are less viewed online than the other top categories. These are a significant source of income for the stations, as Al Noor News owner explained in interview:

> Yes, advertisements, or we can say TV commercials, are the main source of income, so we have our contacts in different advertising agencies from which we get TV Commercial. As on the other hand we [...] make local advertisements on our area. And this TV advertising concept is growing day by day in our area (Noor Ul Islam, 2015a).

Advertisements on the Kargili stations are for mostly for local business as well as the television station's own ads about upcoming shows. Some outside institutions that aim to attract Kargili students also advertise with these stations.

Figure 15: An advertisement screenshot from Munshi Habibullah Mission School, a Kargili commercial on Al Noor News Ladakh (Al Noor News Ladakh, 2014b).

Al Noor News has multiple short video advertisements like this that are approximately a minute long. Figure 15, is a screenshot of such a programme that the station made for a local school. The commercial is a focus on inclusive education, but this is presented for advertising purposes.

Finally, as Figure 10 and Figure 11 show earlier, entertainment alone is clearly not a top priority for the Kargili local stations; while entertaining items such as local music performances are shown they are commonly presented in the context of news or current affair programmes.

The Languages of Kargili Stations

One of the most complex issues to analyse in these programmes is one of languages. There are many different languages that could possibly be used in these programmes. Hindi and Urdu are two commonly used languages spoken in many South Asian countries; they are recognised at the national level. A significant number of people in India speak English, another nationally recognised language, as a legacy from historical British colonism. In addition, more than a hundreds of other languages are spoken in India. On the district administration Kargil-Ladakh website it is written that the languages spoken in Kargil district are "Shina, Balti, Purig, Ladakhi" (District Administration Kargil, 2015). Each of these is a less common language in India as a whole, and generally associated only with the region in which Ladakh is found. Language-based communities can range from only a few thousand members (such as in the case of Shina, Balti, Purig, and Ladakhi) to a few hundred million spreading all over South Asia (as in the cases of Urdu, Hindi and English).

When viewing the programmes on the Kargili stations that are posted on YouTube I began to notice that most of the narration, interviews, and titles seemed to be in Urdu and Hindi, or a mixture of Urdu, Hindi, and English. Figure 16, below, is a screenshot from one of the programmes telecast by Al Noor News Ladakh. There are four different languages are used on the title page: Urdu, Hindi, English and Ladakhi.

Figure 16: Screenshot from Al Noor News Ladakh, 2014 (Al Noor News Ladakh, 2014a).

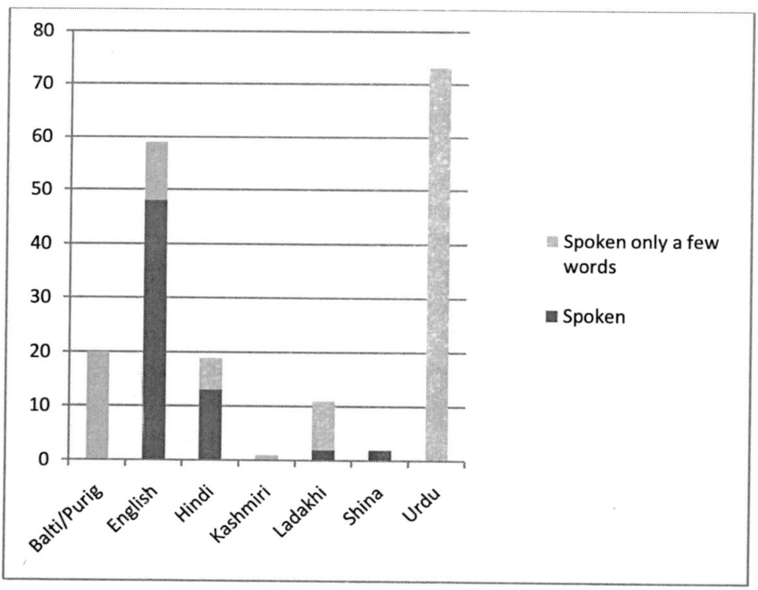

Figure 17: A chart detailing the number of episodes using the different languages in spoken form, both when speaking only a few words and more extensive conversational or narration use.

Three of those languages—Urdu, Hindi and English—are the nationally recognised languages, meaning that local television employs the same languages as larger—state and international—level programming.

In order to more precisely see what languages are used in the Kargili television stations' programmes I performed content analysis on what appeared in both their spoken and written forms, marking which of the following seven different language categories are used in each of the episodes: Balti/Purig, English, Hindi, Kashmiri, Ladakhi, Shina, and Urdu.

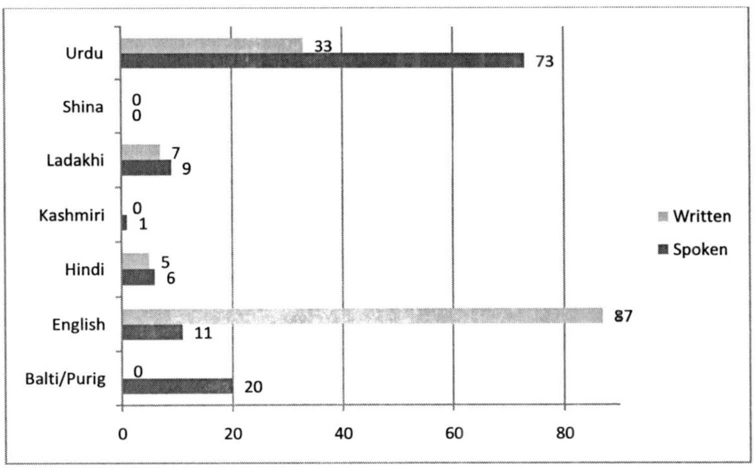

Figure 18: A chart of the number of episodes using spoken vs. written forms of the various languages. Only the numbers from the "spoken" category in Figure 17—where the language is used conversationally or for narration—are included as the "spoken" category in this chart.

As charted in Figure 17 and Figure 18, there are a number of interesting patterns in the language use of Kargili television stations.

Even though Balti and Purig are consider different languages with significant similarities in this analysis Balti and Purig have been combined into one category. Both Balti and Purig are Sino-Tibetan languages, and linguists estimate that Balti is approximately 78-85 per cent similar to the Purig language, which is also spoken in the region (Govt. of India, 2001). According to the Ethnologue languages database, Balti has 290,000 speakers globally (Lewis, 2009). Of those speakers, an estimated 270,000 live in the parts of Pakistan across the border from Kargil, while 20,000 live in India, mostly in the Kargil region (Govt. of India, 2001; Lewis, 2009). Most of these speakers are members of the Balti ethnic group, which originates from these same regions. Balti is most frequently written in the Arabic script, like Urdu. Many Balti speakers also speak Urdu, although reportedly only 3-5 per cent of Balti speakers are literate in Urdu (Lewis, 2009). Purig, or Purik, has about 37,700 speakers, found in and around the Kargil region (Lewis, 2009). Many Purig speaking communities have reportedly shifted to Balti in recent years, and Purig is often spoken as a second language in communities of Balti and Shina speakers (Lewis, 2009). Purig is written in the Arabic alphabet, and a comparatively high number of Purig speakers (61 per cent) are literate (Lewis, 2009). Because these languages are so similar it is hard for a non-native speaker to separate the uses of these two languages; upon analysis it is shown that it is unnecessary to do so as Balti and Purig play similar linguistic roles in the online television shows. As shown in Figure 17 above, both languages have a clear linguistic presence, and roughly 23 per cent of the episodes analyse posted on YouTube contain some Balti and/or Purig. Yet as Figure 18 demonstrates, neither language is used in text, which is somewhat surprising given what we know about both the low Urdu literacy rates for Balti speakers, and the high percentage of Purig speakers who are literate in their own language.

English, an Indo-European language introduced to India by the British during the colonial period, is one of the 22 official languages of India. While a very small segment of the Indian population, only a few hundred thousand Indians, speaks it as their first language there are an estimated 86 million Indians who speak English as their second language, and another 39 million who speak it as their third language

(Govt. of India, 2001). English is commonly considered the language of the urban elite, and is frequently used by media outlets in India. An analysis of the episodes of Kargili television on YouTube suggests that English plays an important and complex role in Kargili television. English is spoken in 59 of the 87 episodes, but in 48 of these episodes it is only used for a few words. This indicates that English is not commonly used as spoken language, but frequently used for isolated vocabulary. At the same time English is used as a text in all 87 episodes, demonstrating that the visuals of Kargili television correspond to global standards. This pattern of language use matches the general language patterns in India, where many educators distinguish between English speakers—those who read and write, as well as speak and understand English in conversations—and English users, who can only read and write English. There are an estimated 350 million English users in India (J. Jenkins, 2014, p. 164).

The third language, Hindi, is another Indo-European language that is one of the national languages of India. It is used in many, but not all, parts of India, and is more common in the northern areas of India. There are a reported 258,000,000 speakers of Hindi in India (Govt. of India, 2001). Although Hindi and Urdu are considered "co-dialects", meaning that they share grammatical structures and vocabulary, Hindi is written in the Devnagari script that is derived from Sanskrit. Hindi is written and spoken in 22 per cent of the analysed episodes, and as shown in Figure 17 it is, when spoken, used conversationally rather than as vocabulary words. As shown in Figure 18, Hindi is statistically almost equally likely to be written as spoken, however this number is misleading in giving a sense of the role of Hindi text in the Kargili television episodes; a majority of the textual uses of Hindi are in the titles for Al Noor News.

Kashmiri is an Indo-European language with over 5 million speakers in India. It is written in the Arabic script, and has a 50-55 per cent literacy rate in the state of Jammu and Kashmir (Lewis, 2009). As shown in Figure 17 and

Figure 18 Kashmiri is only spoken in one analysed episode or 1.15 per cent of the episodes, as part of an interview and is not used textually at all. The relative lack of Kashmiri use suggests that the focus of Kargili television stations is not on getting viewers from other parts of the state outside of the Ladakh region.

In contrast, there is a small but significant use of Ladakhi in these episodes. The Ladakhi language is a Sino-Tibetan language mostly spoken in the Leh and Kargil districts of Jammu and Kashmir, India, although some speakers are found in Himachal Pradesh state as well. There are 105,000 speakers in India and 117,000 speakers globally (Govt. of India, 2001; Lewis, 2009). It is similar to the Tibetan language, with about 53-60 per cent intelligibility between Ladakhi and Tibetan speakers (Lewis, 2009). Ladakhi is written in the Tibetan script, and in its written form is different from its spoken form; only about 20-50 per cent of Ladakhi speakers are estimated to be literate in Ladakhi (Lewis, 2009). Figure 17 shows that 13 per cent of the analysed episodes, 11 episodes, contained spoken Ladakhi, which are almost evenly divided between being used conversationally and as vocabulary words. All of the instances of written Ladakhi charted in Figure 18 are of its use in Al Noor's 2014 logo; Ladakhi is not written for any other purpose in these episodes, which is not surprising given the low numbers of literacy in Ladakhi.

Shina is an Indo-European language spoken by members of the Brokpa (or Drokpa) ethnic group, a group of people who have been popularly exoticised as the "true" Aryans. A majority of Shina speakers, 337,000, live in what is now Pakistan—in the Northern Areas, Gilgit, Diamer, and Baltistan districts—and there are about 371,400 total speakers (Lewis, 2009). In spite of the high number of Shina speakers in Kargil there are only two episodes of Kargili television with Shina, as shown in Figure 17. There are no reports of a written form for Shina, and its speakers, when literate, commonly use Urdu for writing (Lewis, 2009). This explains why there is no textual use of Shina in Figure 18.

The most commonly spoken language in these episodes is Urdu, an Indo-European language with 10,000,000 speakers in Pakistan and 51,536,111 speakers in India (Govt. of India, 2001; Lewis, 2009). Urdu is written in the Arabic form, and as mentioned earlier the spoken version is a co-dialect with Hindi. Some formal and newer terms in Urdu have been adopted from Arabic and Persian, as opposed to Sanskrit in the Hindi dialect. Urdu is spoken in 73 of the 87 viewed episodes, or approximately 84 per cent of the episodes. It is the most common language, and as demonstrated in Figure 17 when used it is for both conversation and narration, as opposed to being used simply for vocabulary words. Urdu has a particularly strong showing as a narration language, and was used by the Kargili news anchors in preference of other languages. While second to English in textual use Urdu still has a strong visual presence in these episodes; it is used in text in 33 episodes, or 38 per cent of the time.

The analysis of local language use was complex due to the commonality of language switching in the media. Sometimes it is hard to distinguish the category of a spoken language because people are constantly using words from different languages—such as Balti/Purig, Shina, Ladakhi, Urdu, Hindi, and English—during one conversation. However, given the data presented there are a few clear patterns. Overall national languages such as English and Urdu have a much stronger presence in Kargili television station broadcasts presented on YouTube, while local languages such as Ladakhi, Balti/Purig, Shina, and Brokpa have a much smaller spoken presence. These results are specific to those programmes posted on YouTube.

Some of my other sources suggested different, although complementary, language patterns for programmes that are not posted to YouTube. The owner of Al Noor explained in interview that, "the whole programme on the news channels use to run in Urdu and Hindi language, but on news time we use to broadcast the same news in three different languages as Urdu, Purig, and Shina" (Noor Ul Islam, 2015a). A journalist working for Kargil Today mentioned that, "[f]or one complete week we show programmes in the local Balti language, the next week [we] show programmes in Urdu. We also have news headlines read in English" (Ladakhi, 2015). S TV Ladakh's director observed, when asked about language use in an interview, that, the station uses "[m]ostly Hindi, [although] nowadays I am using Ladakhi language. Balti, Purig if we have to record Shina than we use the Shina language. We use Urdu also" (Zaidi, 2015a). In another interview one of the senior journalists from Kargil who worked for Kargil Today as a volunteer mentioned that for religious shows they use local languages (S. Hussain, 2015). He argued that it is impossible to make programmes in six different languages, which would be necessary if all local languages were used in the news. He also mentioned that lots of people from outside the region come to Kargil for work, including government officials who do not understand local languages, and since they knew a significant portion of the local population understands Urdu they decided to start using the Urdu language in their local news (S. Hussain, 2015). The interview data therefore supported the results from online analysis that show the complexity of language use, while suggesting some new patterns that might be present in programmes not available online. An emphasis on switching language according to needs—whether set by the format of the show, the show's contents, or the perceived audience of the show—was common in all of these interviews. These results suggest that earlier media language patterns may be changing, as one author wrote that over a decade ago that the Leh dialect of Ladakhi was the standard language for broadcasting in the Ladakh region, and of Ladakh's radio broadcasts (Paldan, 2002).

Local languages are rarely used in texts; when used most appear in interviews and are sometimes translated into Urdu for viewers. As seen, Urdu and English each have their own particular roles; Urdu is used as a conversational and narration language, while English is often used for textual purposes. The fact that English is used as a text in all 87 episodes analysed raises many interesting issues about the role of English in local Indian media. In addition to the colonial influence there are other reasons why English is becoming a popular language in Kargili local media. There are hundreds of words associated with new technologies and institutions—such as computer, internet, mobile phone, and school—that people use on daily bases in both written and spoken forms.

Programme Content

When working to analyse the contents of these programmes I started much like I did in my media category analysis, by defining my terms to ensure that I classified the data correctly. Based on my casual viewing of the media in the past I decided that there were eight different topics I was interested in looking at in these programs. I then developed for each topic a brief list of the types of things I would have to see or hear in a programme for it to count as having that content. The topics, and their general definitions used to direct my analysis, are as follows:

- *Political*- any mention of government, parties, voting, laws.
- *Cultural*- food, clothing, history, dances, customs, traditions (except language).
- *Educational*- schools, learning.
- *Religious*- religions, Buddhism, Islam, Hinduism, Sikhism.
- *Regional*- mentioning Kargil, Leh, or Ladakh as a region.
- *National*- mentioning India or Delhi (capital), referring to national borders.
- *Military*- Indian army, war.
- *Language*- mentioning anything about languages as a topic.

These contents are not exclusive categories; one programme might contain multiple topics and therefore contribute to multiple content categories in the analysis.

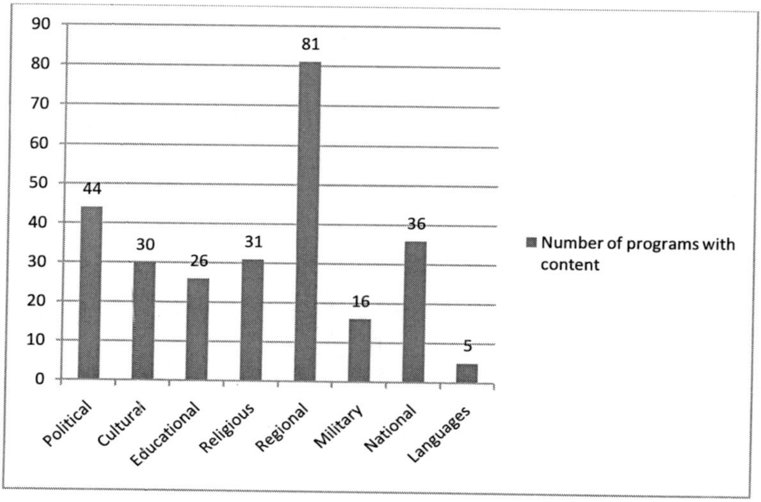

Figure 19: The number of programmes in the Kargili stations posted on YouTube containing the topics analysed.

The results, as show in Figure 19, clearly demonstrate that the local area is the most significant topic addressed on Kargili local television stations; 81 of the 87 programmes analysed included some discussion of Kargil and its surroundings as regions. In contrast, topics such as the military and languages received much less attention. These topics seem like they might be important to local station viewers—the military has a significant presence in the area and languages play a significant role in Kargili identity—yet they are not well represented and were only mentioned in a few episodes. The programmes that contain content related to the military are all in the news and documentary categories.

These numbers about Kargili stations' programming content might slightly change if all the programmes broadcast from these stations were posted online; the analysed programmes are only a portion of all of the programming from the Kargili stations. The exclusion of materials from the religious stations has also impacted these observations as well.

Images and Visual Styles

The videos that are available on internet show that the stations' visuals are varied and communicate the complex role of the local station in Kargil. The styles of programmes telecast by these stations are constantly changing, although it is very common to now use design elements that are similar to those found in national and transnational media outlets. Editing techniques have changed in the past four years; in earlier programmes there is less evidence of editing and narration. Many of the early programmes were simple minutes-long videos that recorded of the events and functions in real time. In the past few years, however, Kargili stations' programmes are getting more complex in terms of contents, graphics, editing, and style.

One important pattern in the visuals is the emphasis on the local region. The Kargili stations' mission of presenting region-specific news is reflected clearly in their visuals. A majority of the programmes, 70 of the 87 or just over 80 per cent, include shots filmed on location for interviews, events, and other reasons. In addition to the on-location video work, 53 of the 87 analysed programmes, or almost

Figure 20: Screenshot from "The Zojilla Issue and the Kargili Peoples problem" (Al Noor News Ladakh, 2014c).

61 per cent of the programmes, contained extra views of the area, establishing shots of the Kargil region. Showing images of local streets, landscapes, and scenery helps to emphasise the importance of the local in the Kargili programmes.

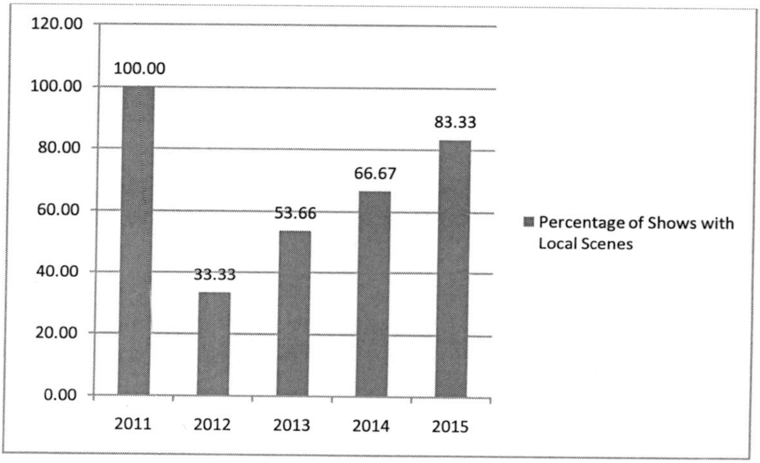

Figure 21: The percentage of Kargili stations' programmes online that include shots from the Kargil region to establish place. These can be scenes from town, roads, pictures of mountains, or other regional sites, and are not directly referring to the main content or narrative in the programme.

As seen here in Figure 21 the percentage of Kargili stations' programmes using visuals with shots of local scenes, landscapes, or other places that are not directly related to the content of the episode has been increasing steadily since 2012. This is ignoring the 100 per cent figure in 2011, as it reflects the presence of the local in only one show. The steady increase suggests the growing significance of the local to Kargili viewers and media persons alike.

There are other patterns found in the post-production graphics in the programmes that might seem to contradict these messages. One is S TV Ladakh's use of opening and closing sequences with a number of representations of landscapes that are clearly not Kargili or Ladakhi—most feature open green areas with rivers and lakes, while one even has a scene with a surfer—included with a few rocky and mountainous landscapes that could, but are not clearly, be from Kargil. The perceived local and foreign landscapes are "flipped" forward as if they were pages in a book we were viewing, moving from the local to the global. The use of this image right before talking about a local ceremony, and showing shots of the ceremony, provides an interesting contrast in ideas of place (S TV Ladakh, 2014). The use of shots of a globe in these same graphics suggests another emphasis on global-local connections as well. S TV Ladakh is not the only show to use such graphics, and similar graphics are present on the shows from the other two channels as well. All three stations use globes in their opening graphics and their opening themes reflect transnational themes.

Another almost contradictory trend is the increasing use of small studios with a green screen, which are being used in newer videos. In spite of the rising percentage of shows that use visuals establish Kargil as a local region, a rising number of shows are also using the green screen backgrounds to create alternative landscapes in the media, particularly landscapes linked to famous cities or companies in other parts of the world. This phenomenon, which suggests the impact of globalisation on Kargili stations, started occurring in the online media in Kargil Today's work. Before 2013 there were no studio shots in the Kargili station programmes, however beginning in February 2013 Kargil Today included studio news with anchors. The station began, and has continued since that time, using studio shots with visual styles that would be easily recognisable to viewers of international channels, including using the green screen to edit backgrounds, and adding scenes from around the world.

For example, in Figure 22, above, two news anchors in Kargil are shown in front of an urban scene which is most probably New York's Times Square. In Figure 23, below, the Kargil Today anchor uses an Al Jazeera studio image as his background.

Figure 22: A studio shot from Kargil Today, 2013 (Kargil Today, 2013).

Figure 23: A studio shot from Kargil Today, 2015 (Kargil Today, 2015b).

These images present interesting questions about why the Kargili stations would like to create visual connections between their media and the places/organisations used on the green screen.

Screenshots from news programmes such as those in Figure 22 and Figure 23 also demonstrate that Kargili stations follow common visual conventions in titling, logos, and other graphic elements. This includes the use of English as an international media language, banners, and a logo mark. This use of recognisable visual conventions connects their productions to national and international media.

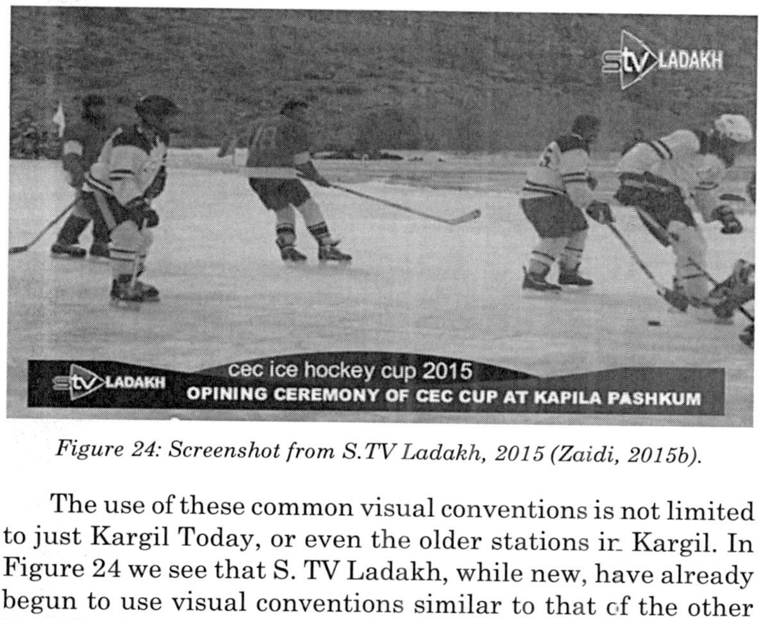

Figure 24: Screenshot from S.TV Ladakh, 2015 (Zaidi, 2015b).

The use of these common visual conventions is not limited to just Kargil Today, or even the older stations in Kargil. In Figure 24 we see that S. TV Ladakh, while new, have already begun to use visual conventions similar to that of the other Kargili television stations. Their logo and titling use English words and standard news style graphics.

A Kargili journalist told me in his interview that viewers in Kargil are used to watching programmes from national and international television stations, and they are familiar with television graphics looking a particular way, which is why Kargili stations has decided to use these graphics in their programmes (S. Hussain, 2015). Kargili local television stations are showing local programmes with transnational programme structure in part, therefore, because of the perceived expectations of their viewers.

Conclusions

One thing that I noticed in the category section of my analysis was the use of the documentary programme. While this was not one of the most frequent types of programmes it is a new programme format in Indian television media, particularly for a local station. In India documentaries are frequently associated with large transnational channels such as Discovery or National Geographic. That Al Noor News Ladakh has produced some documentaries reflects a transnational media influence in programme categories. The station directly links their documentary format to influences from transnational stations. For example in interview the founder and owner of Al Noor explained, "Al Noor News Network is just like Aljazeera, [...] we use to show each and every news like a documentary, and each news reporter has their own project to cover. Which make our news channel very favourite among the public" (Noor Ul Islam, 2015a). Thus, the international influence on Kargili stations shapes not only the type of programmes shown, but the structuring of their work as well. Those involved with Kargili stations believe this to be positively received by their audiences.

Communication is only meaningful, and its effectiveness can only be judged, when a listener understands the narrator. However there are many ways in which "understanding" takes place. In a media context the people of Kargil's local language does not serve simply as a form of basic communication. Language here is playing multiple roles. The use of non-local languages allows the television producers to frame the narrative in a certain way, gives the Kargilis a united front, and provides a medium to address their problems to authorities who do not speak local languages.

All of the stations produce programmes in local, national, and international languages. While non-regional languages had a clear advantage in the online programmes, I was told by the people that I interviewed that local news are often read in local languages also. The clear choice of English as the main titling and text language in all these stations reflects that there is an effort to make their programme understandable to English speakers not only India but around the globe.

The use of multiple languages in one programme is intentional, and certainly from the analysis one can see the benefit of doing this. John W. Higgins, a media studies specialist, argues that the community media movement creates a space for the development and creation of a media mechanism that stays outside the corporate vision (Higgins, 1999, p. 640). He concludes that local media is meaningful as a process, and therefore we must focus on its goals to be successful. As we have seen here the media narratives produced through local media are not focused only on local audiences as idealised viewers; their narrative contents suggest the inclusion of wider audiences than Kargil. If this is true the Kargili local media is created for local Kargili viewers, but also for those outside Kargil, as a public relations tool to present Kargili local views and issues to viewers in other areas. This was echoed in one interview when a Kargili journalist mentioned that the local media came into existence primarily as a way to address the fact that Kargil is cut off from rest of the world for long part of the year and the people of Kargil face unprecedented hardships in addressing their issues to the authorities (S. Hussain, 2015).

The opening themes of Kargili news stations' programmes have familiar national and international themes but the contents and images in the contents are, most of the time, of Kargil thus creating an amalgam of local, national and transnational. This role of visuals in Kargili media brings to mind the earlier discussion of Ginsburg's idea of the "embedded aesthetic"; in studying Aboriginal Australian media Ginsburg suggested that "urban Aboriginal producers working in bicultural settings have embraced an embedded aesthetic as a strategic choice" (Ginsburg, 1994, p. 376). Like the Aboriginal Australians, Kargili media producers have formal training and experience in national and international media outlets. Their visual choices reflect the ways in which they situate the Kargili local media into global networks. The choice of a particular style opening theme or background image is part of a visual vocabulary that they can work with to express Kargili identity in particular ways, similar to the language choices they also make. This process is, as Ginsburg points out in the Australian case, "self-conscious", while these are local television stations the producers utilise the reality that, "the Western aesthetic conventions of the dominant society are culturally available to them" (Ginsburg, 1994). Combined with an emphasis on local images, such as the shots of Kargil, and other visual devices, such as the graphics that all three stations use, bring together local and non-local landscapes, the visuals of globalisation convey a complex message about the relationship between local and global.

Chapter - 4

Media Convergence and the Use of "Whatsapp"

WhatsApp is a cross-platform mobile messaging app that allows users to exchange messages without having to pay for Short Message Service (SMS). As long as they have an internet connection on their phone the users of WhatsApp can exchange messages—including images, video, and audio content— in most parts of the world. It can be accessed through the internet as well as on mobile devices. Users can join groups and share information within that group. WhatsApp also has a feature that allows users to call each other through the app, making it a complete communications platform for cell phone users.

WhatsApp was first introduced in 2009 by creators Brian Acton and Jan Koum. In 2014, Facebook purchased WhatsApp from its developers for the sum of $22 billion dollars (Facebook, 2014). This transaction attracted a great deal of attention to the app and its potential. WhatsApp has become very popular in last few years and the number of users is constantly increasing all over the globe, with a remarkable increase of millions of users every month between 2013 and 2015, as shown below in Figure 25.

Over 800 million people used WhatsApp in 2015, sending 30 billion messages every day (Kim, 2015).

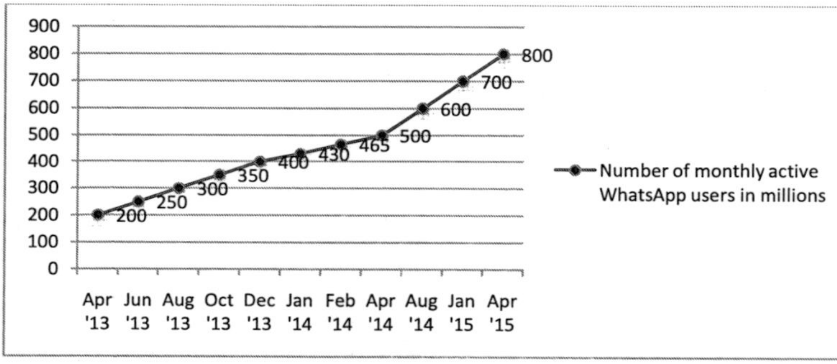

Figure 25: The number of monthly active WhatsApp users worldwide from April 2013 to April 2015 (in millions) (WhatsApp, 2015).

WhatsApp became popular for a variety of reasons. It is simple to use and does not have any advertisements. Users of the app do not have to pay any fee; it is now completely free, although a previous pricing model had it free for the first year and only $1 a year after that. WhatsApp is much more than a traditional SMS. Users are informed about the message delivery, and when the message has been read. In addition to text users can easily send photos, videos, audio, and web links. In some ways WhatsApp is like a combination of a telephone, Facebook, Skype, and YouTube all packed in one app. In many countries, including India, WhatsApp has become a new form of social network (Wired, 2014).

WhatsApp is becoming one of the most popular apps for sending instant messages in many countries, but particularly in developing countries such as India. The number of WhatsApp Users in India is steadily increasing, as it is globally. However, Indian usage of WhatsApp is significantly higher than in other parts of the world. Indian usage accounted for one-tenth of WhatsApp users in the world in 2014 (Business Today, 2014). There is a significant difference in frequency of use, pictured below in Figure 26, between the United States, where only eight per cent of mobile internet users use WhatsApp, and countries like India, where 69 per cent of mobile internet users use it.

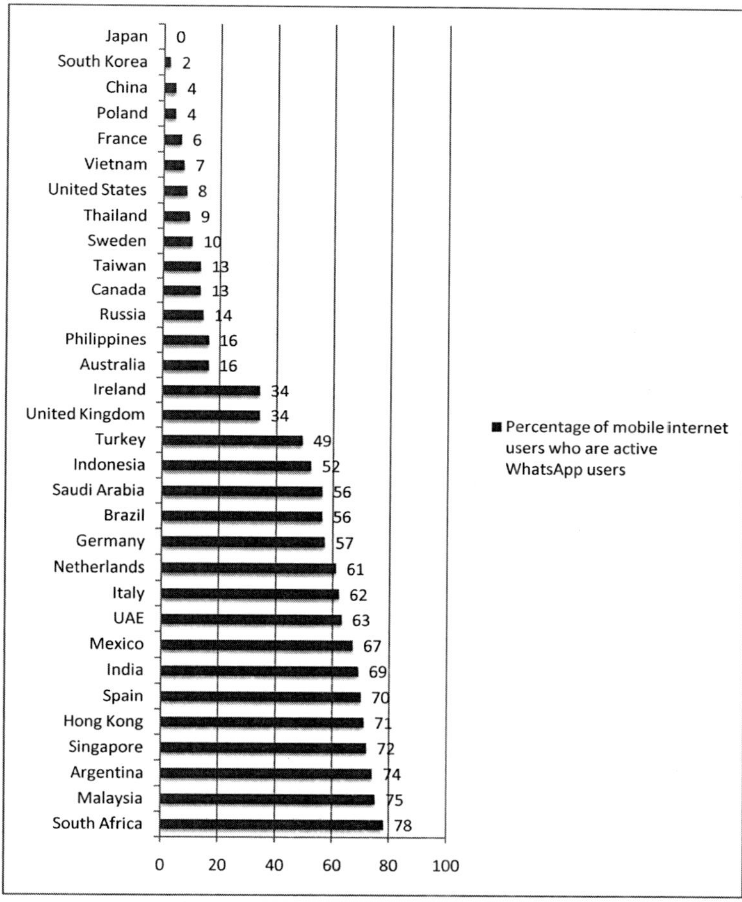

Figure 26: Share of active mobile internet users in selected countries who are active WhatsApp users as of 4th quarter 2014 (GlobalWebIndex, 2014a).

These usage differences are not for WhatsApp only; when contextualised with data that covers other mobile messaging services it is clear that different regions have "preferred" mobile messaging services. In a comparison of the active reach of the most popular mobile messenger apps in India and the USA for the third quarter of 2014, WhatsApp was ranked first for Indian mobile users—with 64 per cent active mobile users aged 16-64 using it—while Facebook Messenger was ranked first for American mobile users aged 16-64 in the USA (GlobalWebIndex, 2014b). While WhatsApp is the most popular messaging service in India, it ranks fourth behind Facebook, Skype, and Snapchat in the USA (GlobalWebIndex, 2014b). The statistics on the popularity of WhatsApp in India are not just dependent on India's population numbers; the most popular messaging service in the USA, Facebook Messaging, has a lower percentage of users for its population than WhatsApp has in India (GlobalWebIndex, 2014b). In fact, the top three messaging services have larger percentages of the mobile market, indicating that mobile messaging in general is more popular in India than in the USA (GlobalWebIndex, 2014b).

There are a number of reasons commonly ascribed to WhatsApp's popularity in India. Many people point to the facts that the app is free and not an advertising platform as major reasons. The technology itself is well suited to developing countries such as India. The lack of high-speed broadband and the high cost of computers in India have made widespread access to internet on computers confined to urban areas only. Slow connections on computers make downloading videos and images on websites such as Facebook and YouTube difficult. But that is changing with the quick spread of high-speed mobile data, making internet accessible to more people in India (Fontevecchia, 2014). The structure of WhatsApp is less data intensive than traditional websites, making it efficient to use. Furthermore, Indian companies are making smart phones that are much less expensive than the international brands. The combination of a cheap smart phone, low cost high speed mobile data plan, and efficiency of WhatsApp has helped people living in far-flung areas like Kargil to be connected to the internet.

Existing Research on WhatsApp

There are few existing studies about WhatsApp and its role as a communication technology. One of the major questions about WhatsApp is why users would choose this technology, and particular app. Karen Church and Rodrigo de Oliveira studied WhatsApp use in Spain, and write that there are different reasons why users choose between WhatsApp and traditional SMS (Church and de Oliveira, 2013). In their research they found that while the low cost plays a major role in adopting WhatsApp, social influence also played a significant role (Church and de Oliveira, 2013). Church and de Oliveira suggest that neither technology is a replacement for the other, as WhatsApp is used for more social and informal messaging while SMS is seen more formal and private (Church and de Oliveira, 2013).

Richard Shambare, a business professor, has written about the role the app plays in poor and developing countries. Shambare writes that in such places the high cost of technology creates a low demand for technologies, creating less access which in the end creates technologically poor consumers (Shambare, 2014, p. 542). In the research done in South Africa on the factors influencing the adoption of WhatsApp, Shambare observes that if a technology is complex and difficult to use then its usefulness to the adopter is significantly reduced, and that technology must also be clearly useful to motivate people to learn to use it. The researcher further argues that adoption of WhatsApp breaks this cycle of technology poverty by being both useful and easy to use (Shambare, 2014, p. 548). Similarly in their research on the app's use in Ghana, Yeboah Solomon Tawiah *et al.* found that polytechnic students in Ghana use WhatsApp for most of their informal communications such as with friends and class mates because they found the app to be cost-effective, reliable, easy, and time-saving (Tawiah, Nondzor and Alhaji, 2014).

People all over the world are using WhatsApp for different purposes. One of the important functions in WhatsApp is creating a group. A user can create multiple groups and each group can have up to one hundred members at one time. Students in developing countries are using WhatsApp as learning resources. Patient Rambe and Crispen Chipunza write that the WhatsApp platform can function as an educational medium in South Africa, one used for bridging access to learning resources, a mechanism for peer-based support, and also to increase meaningful context-free learning (Rambe and Chipunza, 2013, p. 336). Hospital staff and doctors in India are also using WhatsApp to communicate with each other quickly and effectively. In a research done in India on the staff members of an orthopedic surgery unit Pradeep Choudhari found that staff uses WhatsApp for patient care and academic endorsement. According to staff, apps such as WhatsApp save time between the staff members when communicating about a patient (Choudhari, 2014, p. 11).

However, WhatsApp is not always used for applied or positive purposes. In an another study Johnson Yeboah and George Dominic Ewur write about the high usage of WhatsApp among college and university students in Ghana (Yeboah and Ewur, 2014). The authors argue in this article that during their research they found that WhatsApp, instead of making the flow of ideas and information between students easier and faster, was detrimental to the students' work. Students spent a significant portion of their time on WhatsApp engaged in social networking, which led to a reduction in study time, increased spelling and grammatical mistakes in the work they completed while on it, and less attention during class lectures (Yeboah and Ewur, 2014). The Tawiah *et al.* study also found in Ghana that students emphasised WhatsApp use only in informal situations, preferring mobile voice platforms for formal and more detailed serious conversations (Tawiah *et al.,* 2014). Now that WhatsApp can be used for phone calls, a new application for 2015, a new study might bring different results.

Kenton O'Hara *et al.* have looked at WhatsApp from a more symbolic point of view, arguing that the app promotes feelings of intimacy and togetherness among users sending messages (O'Hara, Massimi, Harper, Rubens and Morris, 2014). The authors write that existing models explaining the popularity of messaging apps such as WhatsApp are insufficient; on the surface messaging apps do not seem to offer more than basic communications features found in more traditional electronic communications technologies such as e-mail, and the cost-based explanation does not explain why these particular free apps are popular (O'Hara *et al.,* 2014, pp. 1-2). Significantly, O'Hara's study population in the UK echoed the same ideas as the users in Ghana from Tawiah *et al.* and users in Spain from Church and de Oliveira (both discussed above); WhatsApp was more informal than chatting, more intimate and something done just for fun with friends. They concluded that WhatsApp is particularly effective because it helps users who already know each other to maintain intimacy by connecting their real-world and electronic relationships through quick updates, statuses, and links (O'Hara *et al.,* 2014, pp. 11-12).

These studies provide a particularly interesting glimpse at WhatsApp use globally because they suggest that the Kargili television station's use of the app represents a new role for this electronic media.

WhatsApp and Local Television Stations in Kargil

When I began speaking to owners and producers of Kargil's local stations about my research I was asked several times, "Are you on WhatsApp?" I had been asked that question before by people in India, but was surprised to hear it in the context of discussing television shows. It was then that Kargil Today's owner told me that they use WhatsApp to send their news out to a list of people. Upon my request I was then included on the Kargil Today WhatsApp group, and learned a great deal more about the usage of the app for media purposes.

All three local stations in Kargil have used WhatsApp. Al Noor News Ladakh started using WhatsApp in 2010 and now has three groups (Noor Ul Islam, 2015a). In 2014, Kargil Today started using WhatsApp as well, and the station now has 10 groups. The Kargil Today groups are clearly divided among subcultures of their audience. One group in particular is for students and is popular with Kargili students who are attending university outside of Kargil (Khalo, 2015). Other groups include WhatsApp groups for women and for people interested in religious content. Although S TV Ladakh did not start using WhatsApp until the beginning of 2015, they already have three groups (Shotopa, 2015).

While the ease of use for social and personal applications of WhatsApp are well known, the app is well suited to media applications as well. Technology in not evenly distributed all over the world, and like many technologically poor parts of the world Kargil has internet connectivity problems; thus it is very difficult for these stations to upload their programmes on internet. All three local television stations in Kargil are using WhatsApp to send subscribers news and information, and the app has become an important medium for distributing news. The use of WhatsApp supplements telecasting programmes through cable television and seems to have replaced, for a large part, posting these on the internet on sites such as YouTube.

One of the most basic uses of WhatsApp for media purposes is to quickly notify people of breaking news, as shown below in Figure 27.

The immediacy of the app, that it sends you a notification directly to your phone as a message, makes it well suited to

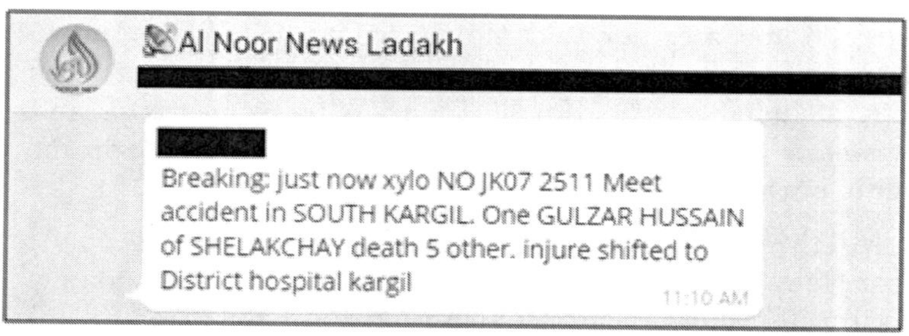

Figure 27: A WhatsApp screenshot of breaking news sent from Al Noor News Ladakh 2015 (Al Noor News Ladakh, 2015c). In each of these screenshots of WhatsApp the sender's personal name and telephone number have been blacked out to respect their privacy.

these types of alerts. Other news stories that are not breaking news are also shared on WhatsApp; there is a lot of information shared in these groups such as weather, sports, education, politics, and religion to name just a few. Specialised local information, such as the school timings and exam dates as shown below in Figure 28, is frequently distributed on the group, demonstrating that this is an ideal media space for local issues.

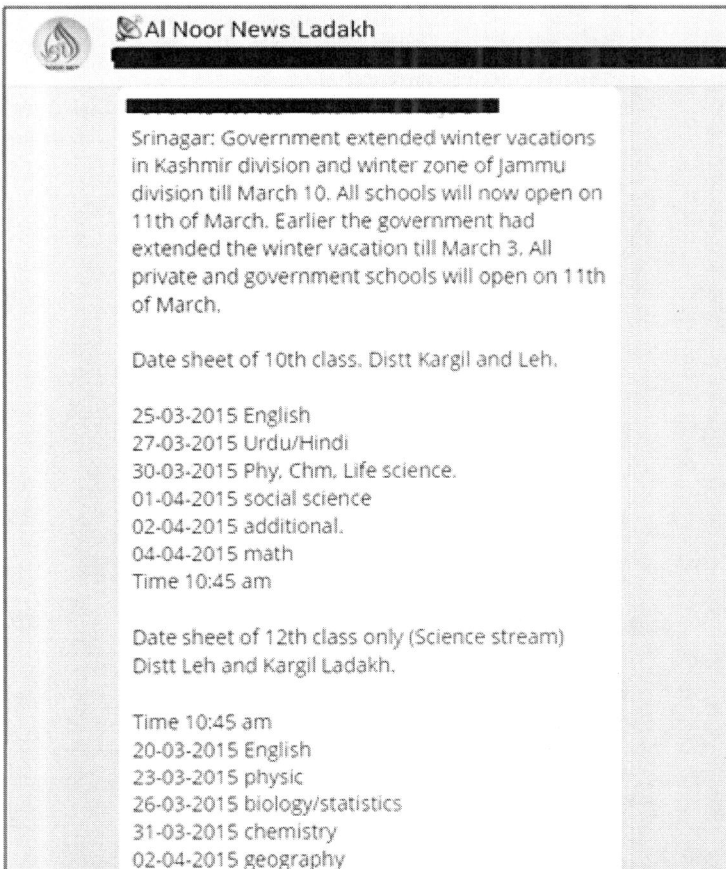

Figure 28: A WhatsApp screenshot showing local news updates from Al Noor News Ladakh 2015 (Al Noor News Ladakh, 2015c).

The app can be, and is, used for many other purposes as well, as shown below.

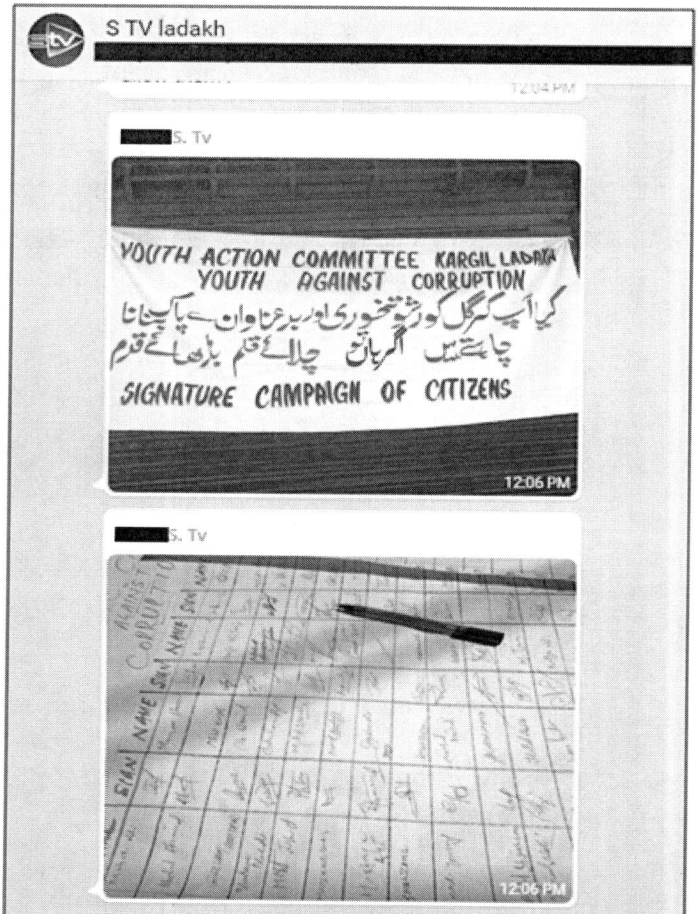

Figure 29: Anti-corruption signature campaign photographs, a WhatsApp screenshot from S TV Ladakh 2015 (S TV Ladakh, 2015a).

As Figure 29 demonstrates, the app is a useful way for sharing images associated with a news story, which can be used both to pique interest and provide more detail. These pictures in Figure 29 are images from a signature campaign conducted by a youth group in Kargil. The campaign is part of a movement against corruption. These WhatsApp messages are both news and a way of providing public awareness about the movement.

Figure 30: Anti-corruption campaign discussion, with photo, text, and video commentary, a WhatsApp screenshot from S TV Ladakh 2015 (S TV Ladakh, 2015a). The Urdu comment reads, "It looks like now our community is awakening".

The contents of Figure 30 screenshot contain common features that are included as follow-up commentary on news stories on WhatsApp. Here people in the group have commented on the anti-corruption story, including images, video clips, and viewer comments/feedback. The television station has also followed up with another photograph. This example shows how the many different features of the app can work together to provide a holistic and interactive media environment.

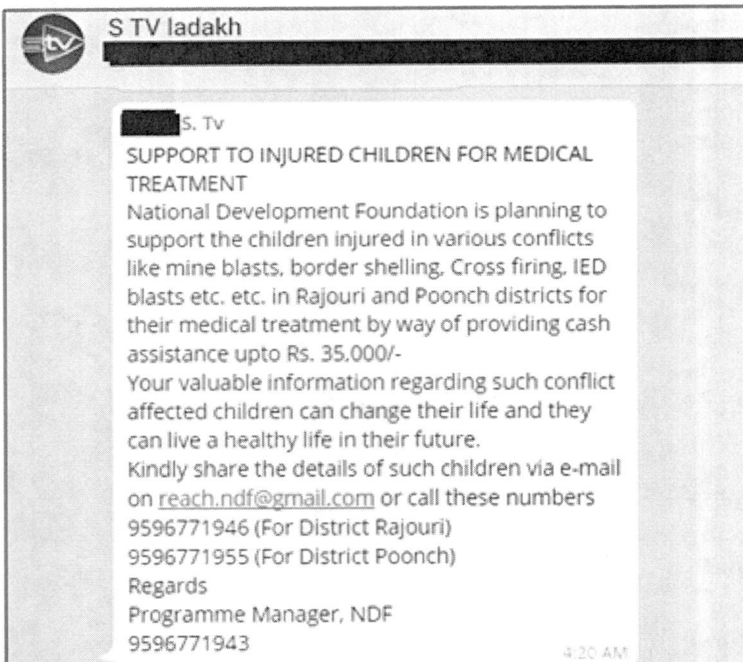

S TV ladakh

S. Tv

SUPPORT TO INJURED CHILDREN FOR MEDICAL TREATMENT

National Development Foundation is planning to support the children injured in various conflicts like mine blasts, border shelling, Cross firing, IED blasts etc. etc. in Rajouri and Poonch districts for their medical treatment by way of providing cash assistance upto Rs. 35,000/-

Your valuable information regarding such conflict affected children can change their life and they can live a healthy life in their future.

Kindly share the details of such children via e-mail on reach.ndf@gmail.com or call these numbers

9596771946 (For District Rajouri)

9596771955 (For District Poonch)

Regards

Programme Manager, NDF

9596771943

4:20 AM

Figure 31: Post to advertise a cause that viewers might be interested in supporting, a WhatsApp screenshot from S TV Ladakh 2015 (S TV Ladakh, 2015a).

Through WhatsApp the Kargili television stations can also reach out to viewers for purposes other than simply telling about news, such as in Figure 31 above, where a message asking for input for a non-governmental organisation has been forwarded for viewers to help the injured children featured in one of the news stories. This post is particularly interesting because it connects a local issue in Kargil, being a border town that has suffered from violence, to a national assistance programme.

WhatsApp has opened another medium for Kargili local media to send their news this is an innovative way to use these medium as media platform. The significance of this medium is best explored qualitatively, through a description of my experiences with WhatsApp and a case study of how a story is communicated on the app, both of which I present below.

Using WhatsApp: A Participant's Experience

After being persuaded to join WhatsApp, and downloading the app into my cell phone, I was initially confused about the role of the app. There was very little information about the app, and no information about the group that I had joined. When comparing it to Facebook, which has pages with an "About" section and a profile page, I was disappointed about the lack of information from WhatsApp. While I was told that I had been added to a television station's list, I could not find out much information about that list. I still do not know the numbers of people involved in the groups that each station has; there is not total count provided and it is impossible to accurately tell how many people actually receive information based only on participation in these groups.

I quickly became more interested in the app, however, when the messages started coming. From the first day I was included in the Kargil Today group I started receiving between twenty to thirty messages daily which included both news feeds from Kargil Today, and group members' comments and posts from other sources. At my request Al Noor News Ladakh and S TV Ladakh included me in their groups and I started receiving news and comments from all three local television stations. I was also receiving news, comments, and feedbacks from the other group members every day, multiple times a day. The level of activity for Kargili local television stations on WhatsApp was impressive, and sometimes overwhelming. Some days I would get sixty messages in twenty-four hours, my phone continuously buzzing with media messages. If there was an important event happening in the region—such as the opening of the national highway after six months of winter or political discussions during elections—the flow of messages becomes nonstop. The constant activity and immediacy of these posts helps to create a very personal interaction with the news, as it inserts itself into my day.

WhatsApp has potential to help communications in Kargil, as the internet services, telephone connections, and electricity are all provided there unreliably by the government. But WhatsApp still depends on these services, so sometimes when the telephone reception is not working in Kargil the volume of message goes down. When the news stops coming from the administrators the role of the news becomes clear for this WhatsApp group; when no new information is coming there is less general activity going on in the groups; people rarely post their own news but rather respond to what the administrator is posting. Therefore, the administrator of the group—who posts contents, monitors discussions, and controls all the function of the group including adding new members or blocking existing members—strongly influences the interactions with the groups. There are a few exceptions to this top-down approach to content, as a few times group members have also posted content from different sources within their comments.

Every day the first messages begin in Kargil's morning time with a long list of links for state, national, and international news, including sports. Figure 32, below, is an example of the first message of the day sent by S TV Ladakh that begins with news headlines and the other two stations have similar formats. In the news headlines there is no special focus on local news or national; international news are also included. Most of the news stories in this post are only titles, or a couple of sentences long, and they may come with a link to stories on other media outlet sites, so that someone who wants to read a complete story can do so. Often local news is then covered in more detail in subsequent posts; this is written by the stations in their own words, and sometimes includes photographs, audio, and videos.

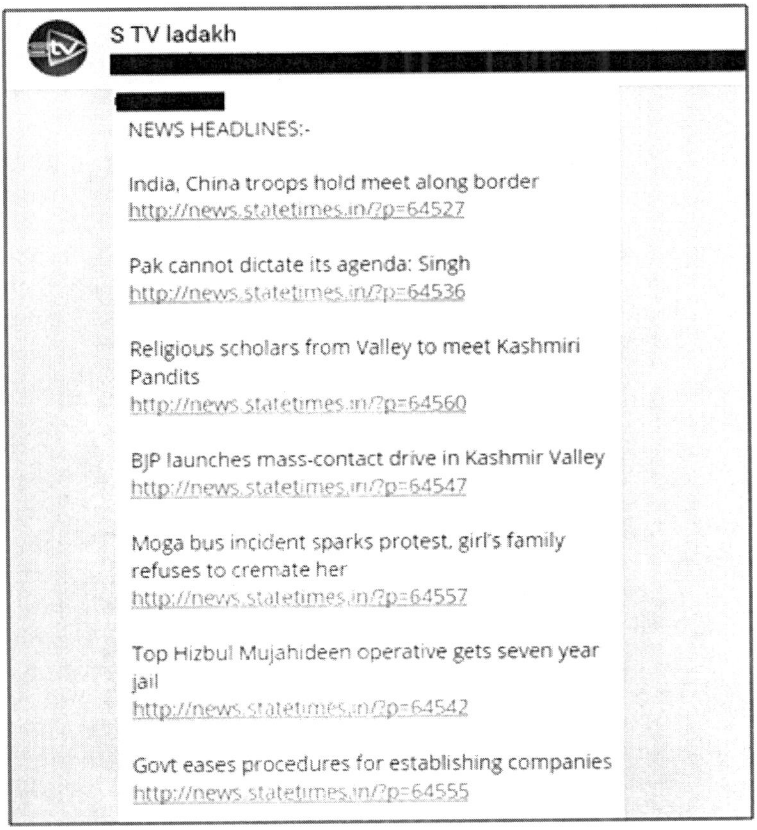

Figure 32: WhatsApp screenshot of the daily news headlines post, from S TV Ladakh 2015 (S TV Ladakh, 2015b).

Figure 33 is screenshot of local news about the ice hockey camp posted by Kargil Today. Even local sports events are covered in detail this way, with photos and videos. All the

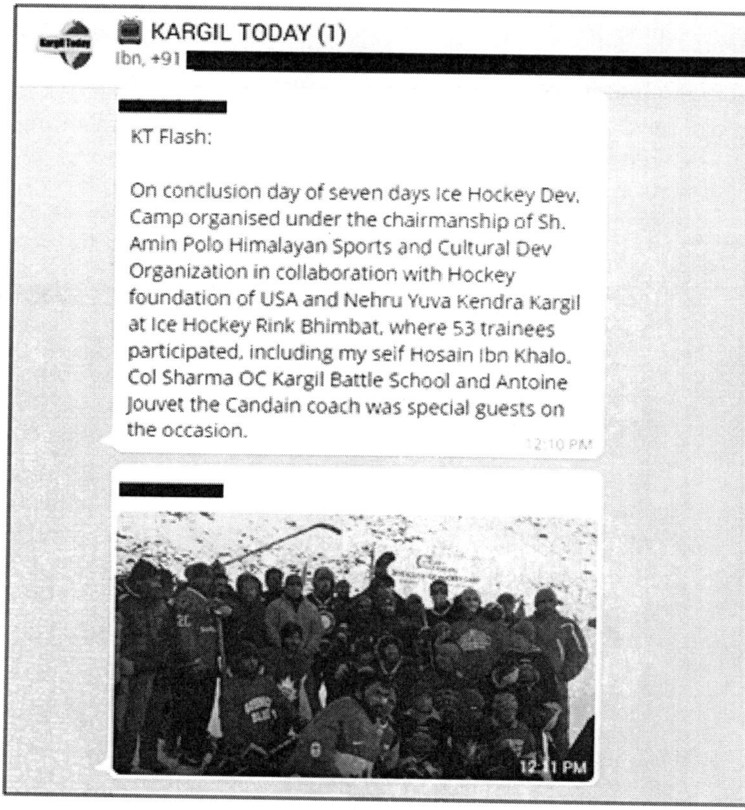

Figure 33: WhatsApp screenshot of a brief summary of a local news story, with picture, from Kargil Today 2015 (Kargil Today, 2015a).

three Kargili stations use a similar format for news on WhatsApp, plain text with additional photos. Often these stations repeat same stories on their different WhatsApp accounts. Group members often comment with additional text, photos, and videos. As mentioned earlier group members also post both local and non-local news; some of the group members are local journalists for print media, as well as journalists for national and international news outlets. In general the posts are friendly and positive, although sometimes the discussion and comments can get a little heated; the group administrator monitors this and controls members from using foul language and unfair accusations. These conflicts in the comments can yield very interesting discussions about news and the media. A few times I have noticed group members challenging co-members for posting graphic photos with their news or posting news that was unreliable.

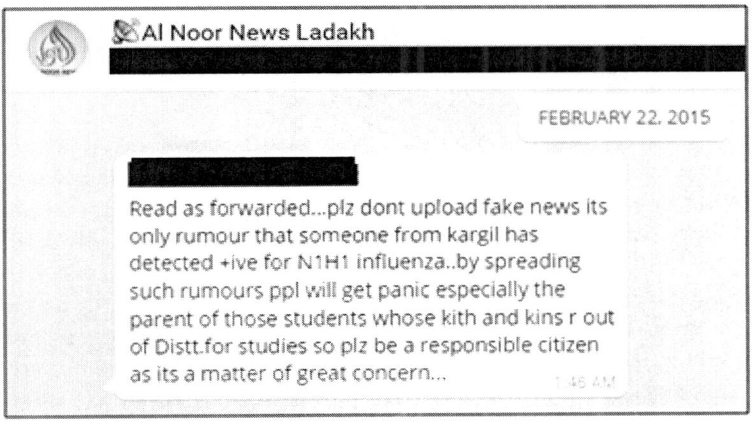

Figure 34: A comment on news that other group members found was not reliable, a WhatsApp screenshot from Al Noor News Ladakh 2015 (Al Noor News Ladakh, 2015d).

For example, in Figure 34 is a screenshot from Al Noor News Ladakh group's page. A group member posted an unreliable story about a Kargili person being diagnosed with "N1H1 influenza" and there was a strong negative reaction from other members for posting this without verifying the story. Commentators like the one above specifically reminded the person posting the news about the potential viewers, the impact that news had on others, and the responsibility of citizens to think of the impact of news on others. Use of WhatsApp therefore gives participants the chance to express ideas, and be critical about, unethical media practices. This ability for both media members and the public to provide commentary on media choices is an important role played by the use of the app.

Those who work at the Kargili local stations are aware that technologies like WhatsApp can be used both for distributing the needed news and for spreading rumors. They are also concerned about the difference in the degree of control they have with WhatsApp. In interview the editor-in-chief of Kargil Today mentioned that in general he tried to stay away from showing controversial news on the television station that can cause problem such as religious and communal violence (Khalo, 2015). The stations can control the contents of their programmes that they telecast, but in social media they cannot always control people's comments and postings, especially when it is public. They still try to balance between control and allowing for discussion on WhatsApp. In the case where a member posted a graphic photo of a motorcycle accident, which was protested by the group administrator and other group members as being an unethical use of images, the administrator encouraged members not to post such material, but did not take it down. But this does not stop members from posting stories, photos, and videos that might deem controversial by some.

Participation in the groups is an important component of membership, and may be enforced. After a few months in one Kargili station's group I was removed from the group; when I wrote to the administrator to ask what I got this reply: "your [sic] one of the silent members in this group. So I revised some silent members without any notice. That's the reason". This policy may be because WhatsApp has a limit on the number of members in a group; if a member is not actively participating the administrator gives a chance to others who want to be in the particular group. This is not always true, however; in all of the Kargili station groups I joined for research purposes I never posted or commented, I was only observing how people are using this inexpensive technology as a news media. After months of silence I was only dropped by one group; I am still a member of two groups run by two different stations.

Case Study: "Stranded at Sonamarg" Story Unfolds on WhatsApp

A case study of one story, and the way that it is presented on WhatsApp, helps to illustrate the news cycle for Kargili stations using this as a media outlet. This is a typical example of how the story unfolds on an important issue in one of these groups. In this case the news is about the reopening of the highway after its closing for half of the year due to snow, and local politicians are trying to help stranded passengers. This was a very important story as Kargilis are completely dependent on this highway for all goods and overland connections to the rest of Jammu and Kashmir; the highway is the lifeline for Kargilis and everyone in Kargil waits for the opening of the road.

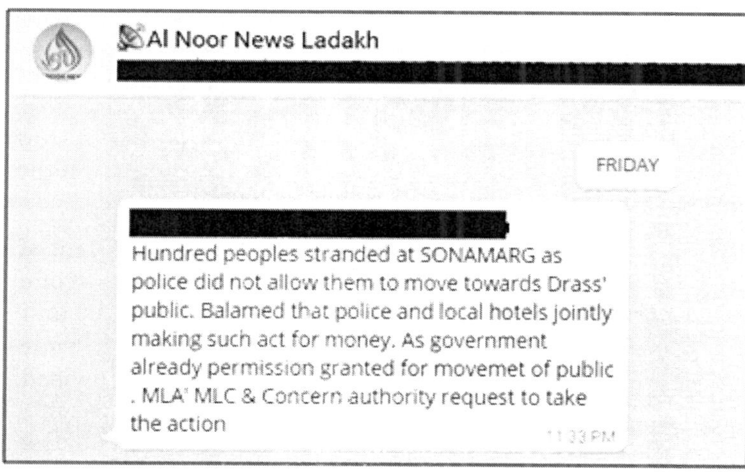

Figure 35: Screenshot Al Noor News Ladakh 2015 (Al Noor News Ladakh, 2015e).

In Figure 35, the first news uploaded was a brief summary about stranded passengers not being allowed to go, and the accusation is that police and local hoteliers are making money from stranded passengers (Al Noor News Ladakh, 2015d). This is a bit more involved than simply a statement of something occurring, as in a breaking news announcement, but it is still a very short news item.

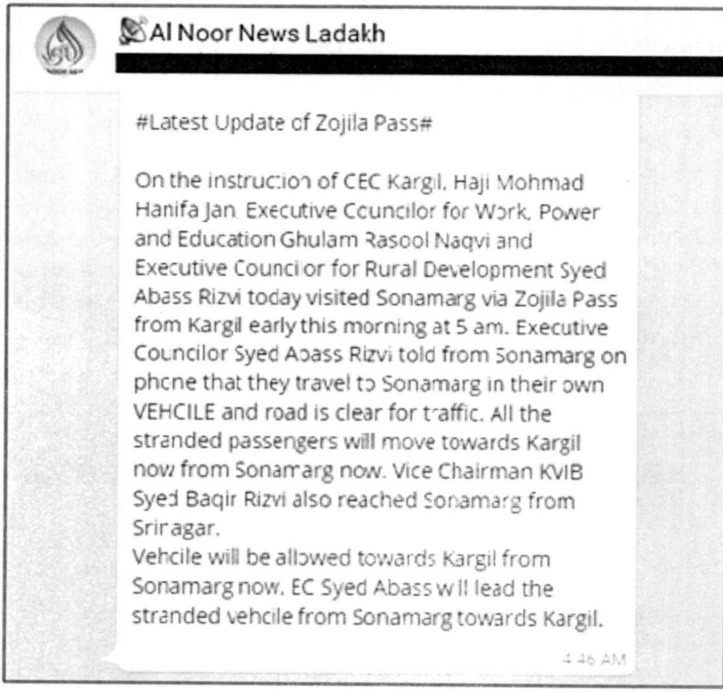

Al Noor News Ladakh

#Latest Update of Zojila Pass#

On the instruction of CEC Kargil, Haji Mohmad Hanifa Jan Executive Councilor for Work, Power and Education Ghulam Rasool Naqvi and Executive Councilor for Rural Development Syed Abass Rizvi today visited Sonamarg via Zojila Pass from Kargil early this morning at 5 am. Executive Councilor Syed Abass Rizvi told from Sonamarg on phone that they travel to Sonamarg in their own VEHCILE and road is clear for traffic. All the stranded passengers will move towards Kargil now from Sonamarg now. Vice Chairman KVIB Syed Baqir Rizvi also reached Sonamarg from Srinagar.
Vehcile will be allowed towards Kargil from Sonamarg now. EC Syed Abass will lead the stranded vehcile from Sonamarg towards Kargil.

4:46 AM

Figure 36: Screenshot from Al Noor News Ladakh 2015 (Al Noor News Ladakh, 2015e).

The next post came about 50 minutes later, with an update on the issue. The text in Figure 36 shows that the Kargili political leaders took the matter in their own hands and went to meet the stranded passengers on the other side of Kargil, and promised that the road would be opened so that all the passengers would be allowed to come to Kargil (Al Noor News Ladakh, 2015d). The story is presented here in relation to the last post. This shows a significant pattern in how Kargili news stations use WhatsApp to share news; important local news are not only communicated in one piece, but with multiple posts going out to viewers it is constructed as a story that has a beginning, ending and all that happens in between.

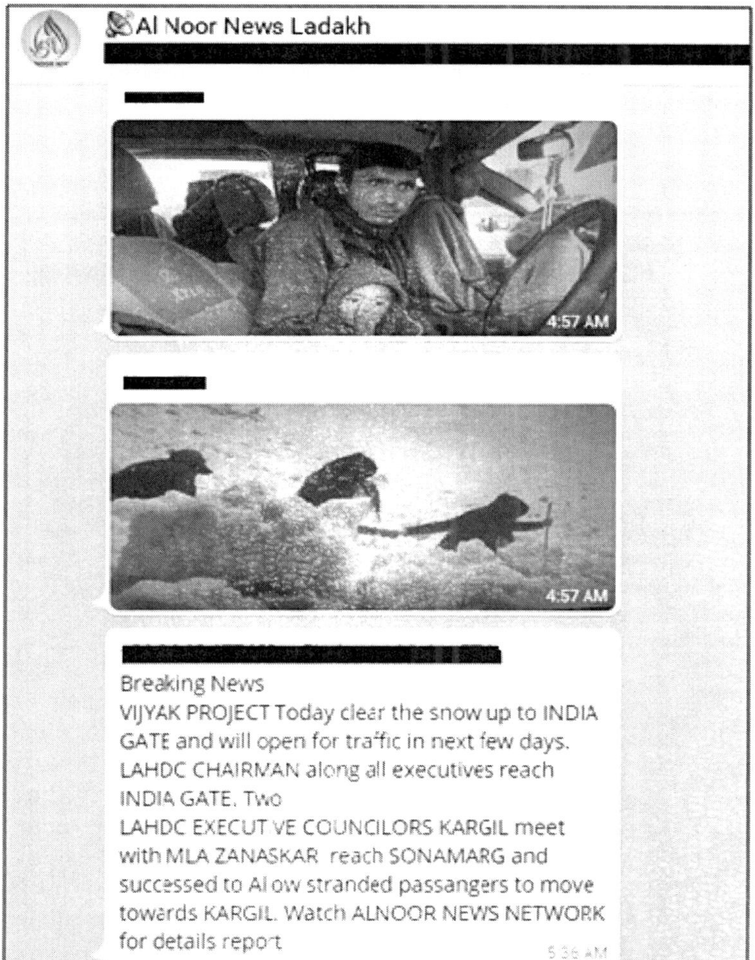

Figure 37: Screenshot from Al Noor News Ladakh 2015 (Al Noor News Ladakh, 2015e).

Next in Figure 37 is a "breaking news" announcement, with two photos of the stranded passengers, including small children; the news is that the road is not yet officially open but for now all the stranded passengers are allowed to travel. The road opening is the most important story for Kargilis at this time of the year, and the news posts on WhatsApp reflect this. The newsfeed becomes more intense; Figure 37 shows that the second news is coming only an hour after the first news and it now includes emotional photos of the stranded passengers' conditions.

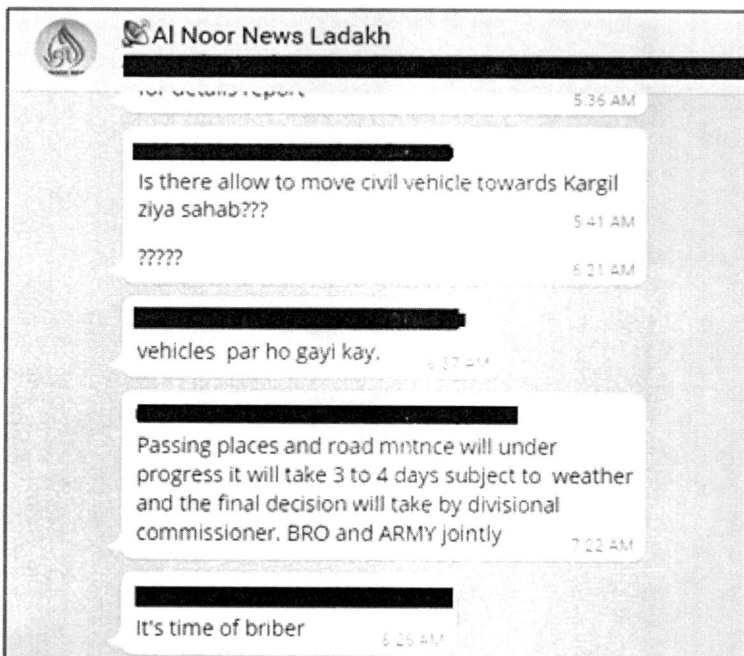

Figure 38: Screenshot from Al Noor News Ladakh 2015 (Al Noor News Ladakh, 2015d).

In Figure 38 the screenshot shows that group members are asking questions about the condition of road, and there is a response from the administrator. One interesting comment in this is that one member wrote "It's time for briber (bribe)" (Al Noor News Ladakh, 2015d). The member is making a sarcastic comment by saying that things only work when you pay a bribe, which refers back to the first news post in this story, in which the author mentioned that police and hoteliers are holding the passengers for money. This post-demonstrates the significance of WhatsApp as a media outlet. Not only can viewers get nonstop news on important topics through WhatsApp; if anyone has additional questions they can post and most often get a reply from the administrator or other group members depending on the question. While earlier posts created a narrative similar to something we might see only occasionally on telecast news, as breaking news for an

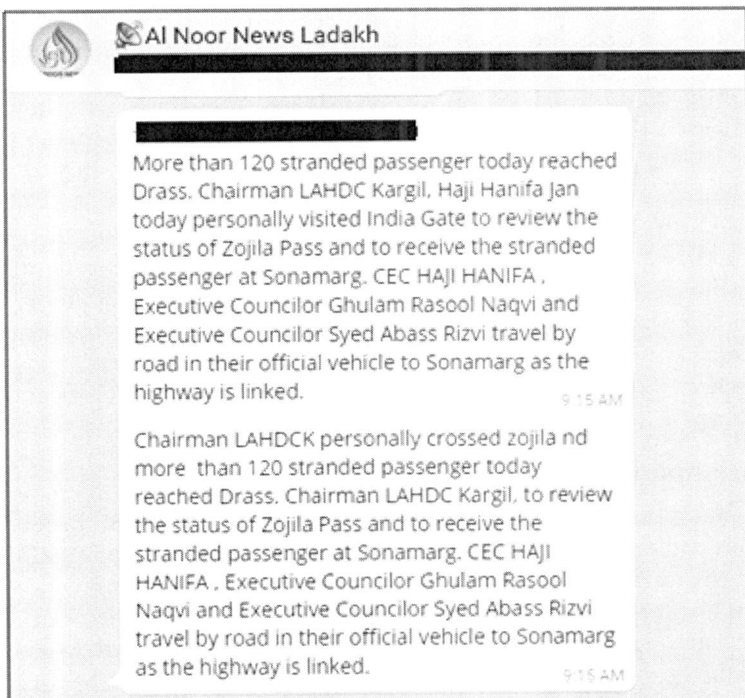

Figure 39: Screenshot Al Noor News Ladakh 2015 (Al Noor News Ladakh, 2015d).

extremely important event, with this post the story has become participatory news where many users can contribute to the information. Using WhatsApp the producers of Kargili local television stations have combined standard news reporting with audience participation in live reporting a new approach.

The news in Figure 39 shows that all the stranded passengers are now allowed to go and they have reached Kargil. This set of information gives an idea of how local Kargili media are using WhatsApp to send news and information quickly to the viewers and how group members participate in the conversation. The entire story unfolds very rapidly on WhatsApp, with new information and news on the same issue coming from different places. In interview the producer of Al Noor News observed that viewers in Kargil like direct talk shows, shows that involve common people talking to authorities. Another person mentioned in an interview that the Kargili stations try to make all their news like documentaries, an in-depth study of an issue, using Al Jazeera's style as an example. The news in this case study and many other news stories posted on WhatsApp are structured in similar ways. The group administrators have combined the hearing of multiple perspectives on a talk show and the narratives of a documentary with the urgent format of breaking news, into a text based media. This format is based both on knowledge of global media formats and local viewers' interests.

Conclusions

Kargili viewers are familiar with both national and international news reporting styles, as are the producers of Kargili news at the news stations. The style of the news—both telecast and on WhatsApp—reflects this familiarity. But there are significant differences in the news due to the way in which these local television stations are using WhatsApp. If you are used to reading the New York Times (or any other globally popular print media) you will not be surprised to see news headlines, photos, and other styles in these WhatsApp posts; these will be recognisable as news. The electronic format is also recognisable as many popular print media are now online or available for subscription on electronic devices. But the use of WhatsApp is more than this. Imagine if you are a member of a group that reads the New York Times together, organised around your interest in the news or membership in a subculture (e.g. student status, religion, or gender). You are constantly fed pieces of the news, and expected to give feedback or otherwise participate, perhaps even inserting your own news into the Times. You receive feedback directly from the Times editors, and items from your group may be shared in other groups. This scenario is far less recognisable as possible with global media such as the New York Times, and highlights the new contributions of Kargili media.

The programmes produced by local Kargili stations are intersections between different screens such as televisions, computers, and mobile phones, part of the concept of media convergence. Jenkins writes that media convergence impacts the way we use media, and happens not only when we use gadgets, but also as in the production of media. The convergence happens in both the companies that produce, and the minds of the consumers. Media convergence thus changes how media is consumed (H. Jenkins, 2006). Media convergence is also about how people use media in different ways from different sources for their own use; this does not always translate into consumer empowerment, however convergence inspires participation and shared intelligence. Jenkins argues that "[c]onvergence, as we can see, is both a top-down corporate-driven process and a bottom-up consumer-driven process" (H. Jenkins, 2006, p. 18). This process is reflected in how WhatsApp has become a multibillion dollar business on the top end, while on the other end are the consumers—such as the owners of the local television stations of Kargil—who are using it for new types of participation. This is an important concept for looking at where use of the WhatsApp app fits into Kargili local media a whole.

There is no specific published data available for the numbers of people watching these programmes and what devices they use to watch these programmes. In interviews with the station employees and owners I was able to get slightly more information. The editor-in-chief of Kargil Today told me in the interview that there are approximately 20,000 people in Kargil watching their programmes, but that the number of people who watch their programmes online is more than 100,000 (Khalo, 2015). He mentioned that 80 per cent of Kargili students go for higher education outside of Kargil, and that they watch these shows online (Khalo, 2015). People in other places, in other parts of India as well as from other countries, watch these local programmes online (Khalo, 2015).

There is also evidence of a varied and active range of ways to access Kargili media. The contents are available through apps like WhatsApp are specially designed for mobile devices. Some of the televised programmes, often in short form, are available on video sharing websites such as YouTube, which offers some insights as discussed in Chapter 3. Many of the programmes that are posted online are reposted on social media such as Facebook by different users. There are comments on the contents of these from viewers on all social media networks. The number of user comments differs depending on the forum; for example, for YouTube (video posting) there are fewer comments as compared to Facebook (social network), while WhatsApp (messaging group) has the most participation by the users. People are using different languages to comment on these shows, and comment on both the media content and delivery. The screen culture of the shows produce by the stations is definitely there, and continuously increasing as Kargili stations are adopting new technologies at a very fast pace.

The producers of news in Kargili stations emphasise the importance of the fact that their stations are community-based, that they consider themselves to be spokespersons of the community. These local television station owners are media activists who are trying to help local communities; they are using their media skills—often gained from working at other, larger, media outlets—to offer a new media service on a shoestring budget and with the resources that require minimal investment. These activists know there are limits to their role, as well as a certain responsibility that comes with it; as mentioned in the interviews they are careful to ensure that they do not cause tension between the powerful authorities and the public but rather serve as a channel in communications between these two parties.

Local stations combine global television styles with community interests in ways that are common for community-based television; however through WhatsApp they also foster user participation. The groups can be organised around viewer subcultures, and monitored to ensure participation. Users are actively engaged while the news is being updated and are part of the news reporting. This style breaks the convention of global news reporting where the viewers have almost no role, except spectator, while keeping the styles of global news reporting intact. This participation is also different from the type of news sharing you might find on social sites like Facebook, where a story is posted, and then commented upon. In WhatsApp the comments are a part of a developing narrative, the meanings can snowball based on the group's participation.

One challenge to the idea of participatory screen cultures with Kargili media might be that these groups are not public, such as a YouTube video where anyone can comment. There are no special requirements to be a member of these WhatsApp groups, theoretically anyone can join the group; at the same time members have to be approved by the administrator, the administrators recognise particular identities as salient to group member (e.g. student status, gender, and religion as mentioned in interview), and groups have limited number of members set by WhatsApp. However, the influence of these groups extends beyond the one group; there are intersections between the different WhatsApp groups. I have noticed that the same stories are reposted in different groups and commented upon by different people. Thus, in the end these stories circulate much more widely, and have the potential to become fully participatory screen culture.

Chapter - 5

Viewers' Perspectives

The purpose of this research study is to understand the role that local television and other media outlets have in India; in the survey I tried to find out more about viewers of these television stations. I designed the questions to learn more about the general public's perception about local media, and to investigate if the local media has a similar impact on different communities.

As required by the university IRB committee there was a consent form with the survey which explained about the investigator, purpose of the study, procedures, risks, benefits, data collection methods, and storage of the survey results. This online survey was only for the people who live in India, age 18 or over; participants were also asked to take the survey only one time. In order to make sure that these criteria were met before taking the survey each participant have to read the consent form and answer five filter consent questions.

- Do you agree to participate in this study as outlined above? (consent question)
- Do you live in India?
- Are you 18 years or older?
- Do you watch television?
- Have you already taken this survey?

This survey was spread by "word-of-mouth" electronically. The first groups of people who receive the survey invitation were in Kargil; in the next phases the survey was sent to people throughout the Ladakh region through emails and social media. In the third phase the survey was sent to people living outside the Ladakh region in all other parts of India. Everyone was encouraged to forward the survey link to other people.

Out of 47 people who qualified for the survey based on the first five questions, only 30 people actually answered the questions; furthermore not every participant answered all questions. For this reason the respondent number for each question is different, and ranges in size between 24 and 30 individuals. Participants were asked to include the zip codes of where they are currently living, which not only helps in mapping out where the participants are taking survey from, but also allowed me to analyse and compare/contrast the data from different regions of India.

Profile of Survey Respondents

All of the survey participants are over 18 years old and all are living in India. When dividing the respondents into age groups I found that 92 per cent of the participants are under the age of 50 and 77 per cent are under the age of 40. These numbers match roughly with the national demographic data, which shows that a little over 50 per cent of Indian population is less than 30 years (Govt. of India, 2011). Overall the respondents are more educated—16 per cent have a high school degree, 24 per cent have a college degree, and 60 per cent have some graduate training—than national averages. The data clearly shows that people with no formal education, of which there are many in Kargil, are not taking the survey. The format of the survey, that it was in English and online, meant that respondents needed to be fairly well-educated—and perhaps even affluent to access the internet for leisure activities—to take this survey. This is one of the disadvantages of doing online survey.

In spite of the fact that the survey was online and all of the comments in comment boxes were written in English, the data indicates that English is not the primary language of any of the respondents, which may also impact the findings of this survey. In survey question #21, respondents were asked "What is your primary or first language, also called your "mother tongue"?", and given a language list of 13 languages (10 of the most common languages in India, and 3 others that are common in Ladakh) and an additional "Other" category where they could write in their own answers. In spite of this variation all 26 respondents chose one of four different languages: Hindi, Urdu, Ladakhi, and Kashmiri. This language question helped to demonstrate that a large segment of the survey participants are Ladakhis; 46.2 per cent of participants wrote "Ladakhi" as their first Language. The percentage of respondents speaking Ladakhi as their mother tongue was larger than the percentage of respondents who said that they were living in Ladakh, only 37 per cent, suggests that a number of Ladakhis living elsewhere in India responded to this study; these Ladakhis living in other places were mentioned several times in interviews as significant consumers of the Kargili stations. As mentioned earlier in this book Ladakhi is only one of many languages spoken in Ladakh, and speaking Ladakhi frequently does not mean that people are literate in Ladakhi. The second biggest group of people in the survey, 34.6 per cent, wrote Hindi as their first language, while 11.5 per cent of the participants wrote Urdu as their first language. In spite of the relatively small number of native speakers here many journalists from Kargil mentioned in their interviews the importance of Urdu as it is understood by majority of the population in North India. A small group of participants, 7.7 per cent, wrote Kashmiri as their first language.

The respondents' locations are an important issue in this survey. My research is about Kargil, which is a part of the Ladakh region, and the title of the survey specifically mentions Ladakh. Also the first recipients of the survey questions were all Ladakhis. The data shows that more

Ladakhis are interested in the subject of local television than people from other areas of India, which would also impact the portion of contributors that came from Ladakh. A large number of Ladakhi students study and live in Delhi, which is reflected in the survey results as the two main geographic concentrations for respondents were the Ladakh region (37 per cent of respondents) and Delhi (33 per cent of respondents). The majority of Ladakhi participants are from the Leh district; only a few living in Kargil took part in the survey. So when looking at the data it is important to be aware that when discussing numbers for Ladakh we are in fact looking at part of the Ladakh region in which media context has very few local options as compared to the Kargil district. Leh district has no private local television stations beside the government-run Doordarshan Leh station, which shows local programmes in the local language (Ladakhi). These participants are thus particularly interested in having local television stations.

The people who took part in this survey are also clearly interested in television media. A majority of the participants, 77 per cent, mention that they watch television more than once a week, although only 37 per cent write that they watch daily. These numbers match with the expected viewing patterns of contributors based on the interviews. I was told in interviews that television is a significant source of entertainment and news, while internet in India is mostly concentrated in urban areas and remote places like Ladakh do not have a reliable high speed internet service. Television watching rates may be even higher among people in India who did not take this survey due to illiteracy. One of the journalists from Kargil mentioned in his interview that not everyone in the Kargil region can read and write, but that using television and radio as a main source for news and information does not require the audience to be literate.

News Sources and Choices

In Question 3 of the survey I asked respondents, "Of the following sources you might hear news from, please rank the places where you are most likely to get your news from, with 1 being the most likely and 5 being the least likely. (1= Most likely, 5= Least likely, numbers will reorder list as you enter preferences)". The four choices then prompted them to rank, from most to least likely the following as sources for news: internet, television, newspapers, and friends. In total 27 respondents answered this question.

I included this question in the survey to find out about the main medium people use to get their news. This helps me to understand if there is a great variation between internet users and other mediums such as television and newspaper. The reason for including the choice "friends" on the list is because, as I have discussed in my earlier chapters, local television stations are making their news available on the internet through WhatsApp and those news are being shared on social media as well as through other social networks. The results, as shown in Figure 40 and Figure 41 below, demonstrate that internet was the most likely source for the respondents' news, and friends were the least likely source.

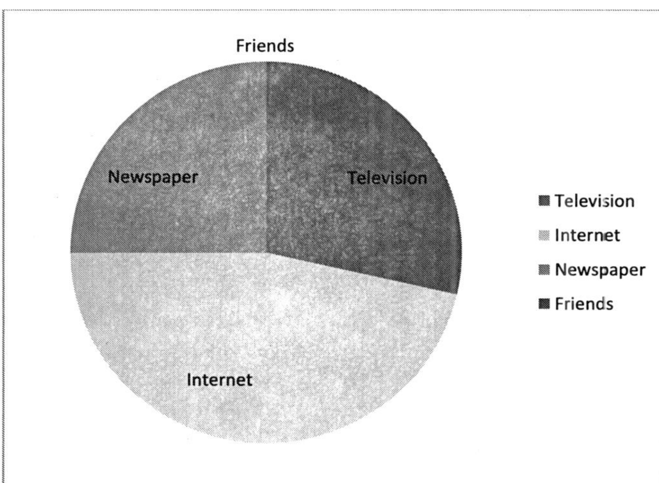

Figure 40: The percentages of survey respondents who chose "most likely" for the labeled choices when asked in Question 3 to rank the choices.

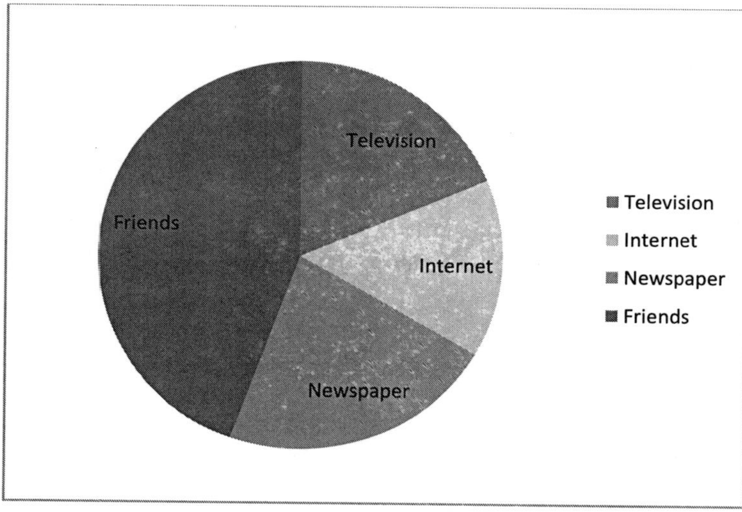

Figure 41: The percentages of survey respondents who chose "least likely" when asked Question 3 when asked to rank the choices.

The ranking of internet over television for news is not surprising. As mentioned earlier, in the last few years the number of internet users is rapidly increasingly as mobile internet is becoming accessible to people living in the far flung areas in India. A number of companies are in competition with each other in India to cash in on the spending potential of India's huge population, and racing to provide mobile internet. These companies, both international and domestic, are also producing cheap smart phones for the public's use. This has helped consumers in India to use their mobile phones, which a few years ago were only used for talking, as replacements for more expensive computers. On the internet people are reading news, and also sharing news through social media and apps such as WhatsApp, as discussed in the last chapter. This has not completely replaced television, which is still the second most likely source for news in this survey, and television is still used as the primary medium to get news in many places in India. While newspapers and friends were ranked as overall "less likely" sources for the news is it significant that they still have some presence; as shown in Figure 42 below all of the categories ranked above the baseline "least likely" score. Furthermore, the categories presented here are not mutually exclusive; people who use the internet may also be using television, as video clips, newspaper, on the paper sites, and friends, through social networks.

Looking at the data for Question 3 in this form, however, does not give all of the information that can be gained from analysing the answers. I also sorted answers by region, to compare the types of answers coming out of Ladakh and Delhi. We might expect that Ladakh, with poor internet connections and limited electricity access would have a lower rate for the likeliness of using internet for the news compared to Delhi; this, however, was not the case as shown in Figure 42 below.

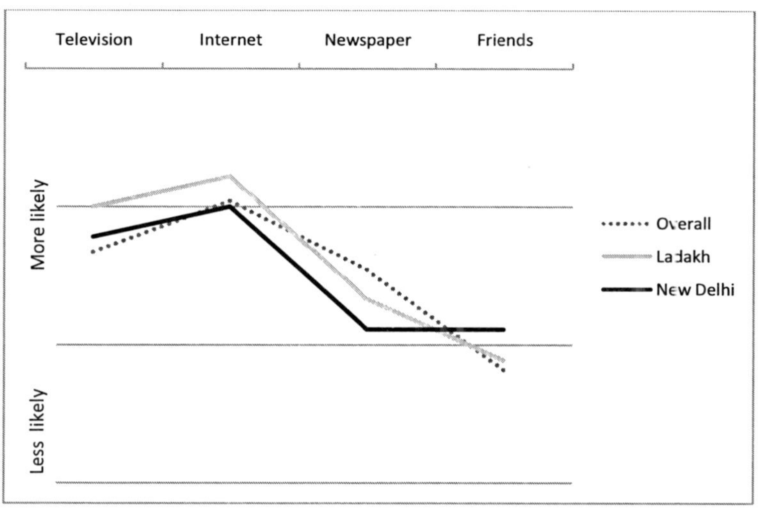

Figure 42: A comparison, based on data from Question 3, of where respondents are most and least likely to get their news, comparing results from respondents in Ladakh, New Delhi, and in the overall survey results.

There are multiple reasons why the Ladakhi use of internet might be more likely than that in other parts of India, including in Delhi. First, in Ladakh electricity is often provided only for a few hours a day, rather than continuously for 24 hours. Households are on a rotation to receive power on certain days at certain hours. So it is impossible to watch television any time you want, or even regularly at a set time. Internet access allows people to access the news according to their own schedules, and chargeable devices such as smart phones mean that viewers are not restricted by electricity availability. Mobile internet is cheap, easy to use and can be accessed anywhere; as in the Kargil news case internet use sends news to people continuously through apps. Getting news through the internet also provides the option to customize news to specific interests, and saves time.

A majority of participants write that while they are most likely get their news from internet they are least likely to get it from friends, and Ladakhis report that they are even less likely to get news from friends than those in Delhi. It would have been helpful to add another question to find out what specific sources the respondents use to find the news on internet; they may not be thinking of friends as a likely source, but might in fact be using social media within the internet category. In a write-in comments section at the end where respondents were asked if local media was important of the Ladakhi participants wrote, "Yes to some extant [sic] as [local media] will give specific [information] but now the role has been taken by social media such as 'Ladakh in Media' through internet". This shows that people are indeed using social media on the internet for their news.

Media Technologies

In order to examine this issue from a related perspective I also asked, in Question 8 of the survey, "Which of the following devices you usually use to watch television shows?" This is a very similar question to Question 3, but it focuses on technologies of access rather than media forums, and asks about "shows" in general, not just news. This question was included in the survey to find out if there is a significant switch in devices to see television shows now as the internet is becoming more accessible in India, especially mobile internet.

While respondents has said in answer to Question 3 that they were more likely to use the internet to access news, in answer to Question 8 a clear majority indicated that they usually watch television shows on televisions as it shows in Figure 43 below. The high numbers of people who selected television may suggest that television is used more for entertainment, as the term "shows" encompasses more than just news. It also highlights patterns of technology usage; if someone is able to watch television on their computer or smart phone it is highly likely they can access the technology to watch it on their television, but the same does not hold true in reverse. Also, since the question specifically read "television shows" some people may have exclude video content that was exclusive to the web or apps.

Since the 1980s, when television dramas started appearing on televisions in India, television has become a major source

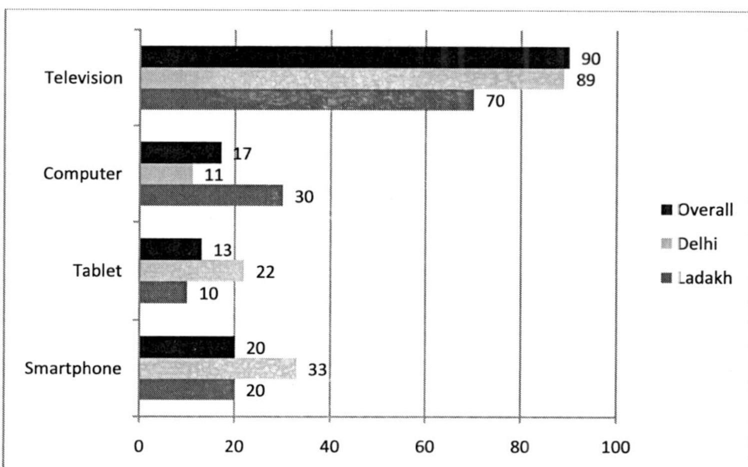

Figure 43: Percentage of respondents who selected each technology when asked to identify the devices they use in Question 8.

of entertainment for millions of people in India. There are now hundreds of thousands of television shows that are made in India in different languages. While some television content is available in other formats, most is not; in India most Indian television shows are not available for live streaming. Watching the few shows that are available online, mostly from international channels, is difficult on both computers and mobile devices because of slow and intermittent internet connections. Furthermore the high cost of computer and electronics equipment keeps many Indians away from computing technologies. The survey clearly shows that, in comparison to Ladakhis, people in Delhi are using more advanced technologies such as tablets and smart phones. One of the reasons for this is that newer technologies reach big cities like Delhi much sooner than small towns.

Languages and Viewers

In addition to Question #21, about the respondent's mother tongue, I also asked in Question #11, "In what language(s) do you listen to television programmes? (Click all that apply)". The respondents were given the same 13 languages—India's ten most common languages and three others that are common in Ladakh—as possible answers. While there were only four mother tongues selected as answers in Question #21 there were six different languages selected as viewing languages; Ladakhi, Hindi, Urdu, and Kashmiri were shared answers, while English and Punjabi were added as viewing languages. The patterns of viewing languages analysed by region as well as overall, yielded some interesting insights.

Many of the answers to Question 11, as shown in Figure 44, are not surprising. The Delhi viewing population, of whom 77.7 per cent list Hindi as their mother tongue, over whelmingly watch news, at a 100 per cent rate, in that language. A majority of the programmes produced by the national television stations in Delhi are in Hindi; even many major international channels have programmes in Hindi in India. This pattern will help explain later in this chapter why a majority of respondents from Delhi show no interest in

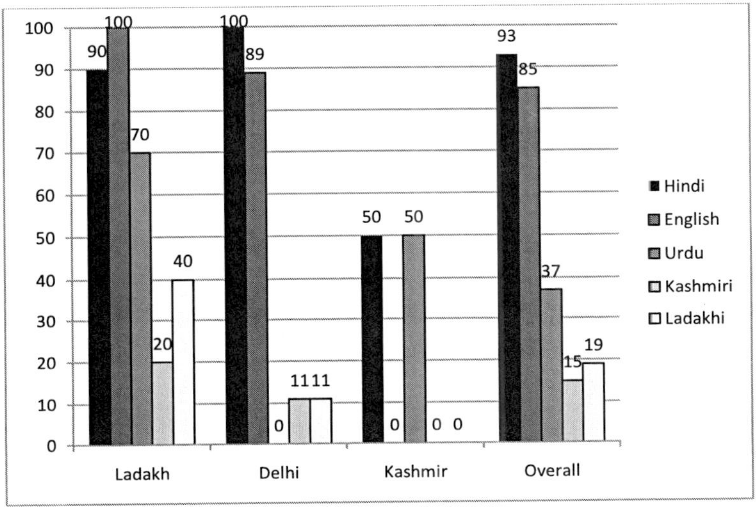

Figure 44: The percentage of respondents that selected the five most common answers to Question 11, grouped by region as well as overall. Percentages of respondents for each answer have been rounded up to the nearest whole number.

having more local stations, which is often associated with meeting local language needs. English was a close second for viewing languages among this urban community. The small percentages of Kashmiri and Ladakhi viewers in Delhi suggest the presence of minority communities living in the capital; data from Question #21 (mother tongues) and Question #19—"Where were you born?"—supports this conclusion.

In contrast those answering from the Ladakh region, where 100 per cent have "Ladakhi" as their mother tongue, only 40 per cent answer that they watched television programmes in Ladakhi, their mother tongue. Opposed to the number of local television stations in Kargil, Leh district does not have too many local television options. In Leh there is only one government run television station that produces local programmes for a limited amount of hours. The lack of options for local stations in Leh causes most people to watch programmes in English and Hindi, which are abundant and are easily available. The slight preference of English programmes over Hindi programmes is interesting, as it might indicate a preference for international programming in Ladakh, compared to a preference for national (or nationally orientated international programming) in Delhi. The third most selected language for television viewing in Ladakh is Urdu, which ranked higher than Ladakhi. As mentioned earlier in this book Urdu is the principal spoken language of the state Jammu and Kashmir, in which Ladakh is located. The state influence is significant, and can be seen in the contrast with Delhi, where no one chose Urdu as a viewing language.

The numbers for Kashmiri are interesting, but since they only represent two respondents it is important not to overestimate their significance. In spite of the fact that both respondents in Kashmir selected Kashmiri as their mother tongue, neither selected Kashmiri as a viewing language. Neither respondent also identified English as a viewing language, which is otherwise a popular choice. In the answers for Question #12 (identify a local station), however, respondents from Kashmir mention the name of a local channel and a Doordarshan local branch, both of which produce programmes in Kashmiri. We know then that the Kashmiri respondents are aware of local language choices even if they themselves do not view them.

The Significance of Local TV

When asked in Question 9, "What are your three favourite television stations?" respondents overwhelmingly answer with either national or international channels; as shown below in the table in Figure 45 the top 10 most frequently listed answers do not include local channels. In fact, no local channels at all are mentioned in the 35 different channels that respondents named.

	Preferred Channel Overall	***Preferred Channel in Ladakh***	***Type of Channel***
NDTV	9	4	National
Colors	5	2	National
Zee TV	5	0	National

(Contd...)

HBO	3	1	International
Sony	3	1	International
Star Plus	3	1	International
National Geographic	3	2	International
Discovery	3	3	International
Doordarshan	3	1	National
Times Now	3	1	National

Figure 45: The top ten preferred channels in response to Question 9, out of a total of 35 different channels mentioned by survey respondents.

Out of the total 35 channel mentioned by respondents 67 per cent are international channels and 43 per cent are national channels. These overall mentions seem to indicate that the respondents prefer international channels. However, there are multiple mentions of several channels, particularly national ones, so when counting each mention of the channels a preference for national channels is suggested; 46 per cent of the channels mentioned are international, while 57 per cent of them are national. New Delhi TV (NDTV), a nationally based channel, is clearly the most popular choice for all of the respondents.

In Ladakh these results—comparing mentions of different channels and the frequency of mentions of each channel—more closely resemble each other. There 60 per cent of stations listed are international, while 40 per cent of them were national; including multiple instances of the same channel 55 per cent of all favourites listed were international and 45 per cent were national. The numbers are therefore reversed in Ladakh.

Another question asked to gauge the significance of local television stations in Ladakh, as well as the rest of India, was Question #12, "What are the names of three local television stations in your area?" The assumption in asking this question was that if local channels were important then people would be able to list their names. If this assumption is correct then local channels did not play a significant role for the respondents. A majority of the people answering mentioned national stations, and some even named international stations such as BBC, in answer to this question. No respondent mentioned any of the Kargili stations in this study, and the local stations listed are mainly the local affiliates of larger national stations, such as Doordarshan Leh. One respondent identified a local station, the Kulgam City Channel in Kashmir. Another person simply wrote in the box provided for station names, "I don't watch local stations". While some trends in these answers—such as not mentioning the Kargili stations and mentioning a Kashmiri one—can be explained by the fact that a vast majority of respondents did not come from Kargil, others cannot, and raise more questions. Does this data mean that local channels do not matter to a majority of people in India? Why would someone even mention BBC when asked about a local channel? And why would a national station such as Doordarshan be included as well?

The interviews that I conducted with television viewers in Kargil help to answer some of these questions. In multiple interviews that I conducted with the television viewers in Kargil about the local stations their first comments were to compare local television stations with national television stations and programmes. I was told by Kargili viewers that local television stations in Kargil are actually not popularly classified as television stations because the general perception of what they do is that they record a programme on a video camera and broadcast that programme through cable. Most Kargili viewers, and by extension viewers in Ladakh, have the idea that for a channel to be an actual "television station" programmes should be broadcast through satellite, and have a full-time staff working and producing programmes continuously. Kargili local stations were not currently meeting these criteria. Viewers and owners of local stations both mentioned the limited resources Kargili television stations have; most often the people who work in these local stations are volunteers who are either just doing it for fun or want to get some experience in the field. Many of these are students. The stations therefore are often not conceptualised by viewers as formal channels, and therefore not listed as "local television stations".

Another reason for these answers is the significance of the role of language in creating ideas of what qualifies as "local". The Government of India owns the national television station Doordarshan, but has created regional broadcasting sub-stations that produce local programmes in local languages. In Ladakh there is only one Doordarshan broadcasting station, which is located in the Leh district, known as Doordarshan Kendra Leh (DDK Leh). Many people called these regional Doordarshan stations local stations because they show locally produced programmes—often heavily censored and scripted by the government—in local languages. Similarly the only reason I can find for someone calling BBC a local station is language; in addition to English the BBC also produces programmes in many different regional languages. Regional BBC broadcasting also contains region-specific content too. The BBC Urdu service is broadcast especially for south Asians, and although it is actually broadcast internationally the role of Urdu as a regional language may cause viewers to perceive it as a local channel.

In answer to Question #13—"Do you think your region needs more local television stations or fewer?" —the overall answers are very close in response rates; 56 per cent of respondents say more, while 44 per cent say fewer. Given the small response number for this question, 27 people, the distinction is not significant. However, when the answers are analysed by region we see a significant distinction; 90 per cent of respondents in Ladakh say more, while only 11 per cent in Delhi say more. One reason why the Ladakhi respondents want to have more local stations is that in the Ladakh region almost all of the locally owned television stations are in Kargil. Leh district, where a majority of the Ladakh respondents live, has no local television station beside the Doordarshan one. So the survey participants from Leh, or people of Leh living outside Leh such as students, want to have local stations that produce programmes just like the Kargili local stations are doing. Ladakhi respondents have a nearby model of local stations, and want the same. It was clear in interviews that people want to know what is happening in their home town, and that the Kargili local stations provide that news to the community; the Leh respondents are aware that Kargili stations cater to people needs by focusing on news and events that are happening in Kargil. Viewers from Ladakh are concerned about the preservation of their culture and in comments indicated that they see television as an important medium to bring awareness on this issue.

In the comments section for the question about whether more local television is needed, the respondents in Ladakh raised few key points. They stressed the importance of local television for particular objectives, writing that local television was necessary "to preserve culture and pass on precious customs in culture to next generation. Also to make aware of ongoing issues in the region", and to "make people aware in every field of regional importance." One individual wrote that they wanted local television, "so that everyone should know all about activities, culture etc. as our country (India) [sic] is too long". A few respondents had more general interests in local television, such as "because we will get to know that what is happening around us", and "to spread more awareness". Others contextualised the need for local television with information about the current lack, writing "there is just one channel at the moment", and "because there are hardly any local station in Leh". The lack of media was considered so important that one respondent wrote, "even if the existing function for 12 hours that's enough".

So the participants of Ladakh agree that local television stations can be a good source of information and news for people of Ladakh, as well as local advocacy sites. They also emphasise that Leh district does not have enough of these outlets, and need more. This hope is reflected in interviews with the Kargili local television owners, who mention that national and international news organisations does not cover regional news, which is why their local stations are becoming popular in local population.

In contrast, in Delhi—the capital of India—an overwhelming amount of news is already telecast about Delhi and there are hundreds of stations—local, national and international—that are based in Delhi. Delhi has acted as the centre for television programming in India was practice from the beginning; Mankekar writes that opposition politicians and television viewers from different parts of India complained about "Delhi centric" programmes when broadcasting first began in India (Mankekar, 1999, p. 61). Local and national stations in the capital carry the same news, and show their programmes with countless advertisements. Many of the Delhi participants therefore have unfavourable views about programmes produced by the local television stations. The one positive comment about the need for more local stations in Delhi mentioned that it could produce more competition. Otherwise the written responses from Delhi were negative. They included the following comments about having more local stations: "Actually...the stations generally cater to all our entertainment needs so we don't need more stations", and "We already have many".

In general, Delhi residents have low expectations in terms of the quality programmes from national and local stations; they see television from these stations as a product selling medium and sensationalised news. This is why one respondent wrote that local television is, "the same content played on every channel with immense advertising", and another complained that "useless and repetitive news on numerous news channels morph or sensationalise [sic] news. It clogs TV systems." In spite of the contrast with answers from Ladakh we can see here that people throughout India are interested in seeing local content that is meaningful and related to their daily lives.

This is clear in the answers to a related question, Question #14, where I asked the survey respondents, "Do you think local television stations are important?" Overall 74 per cent of the respondents answer "yes" to this question, while 15 per cent answer "no", and 11 per cent "not sure". When analysed by region the results seem, at first, to contradict the answers to Question #13 above, as shown in Figure 46 below, which compares the answers to the two questions.

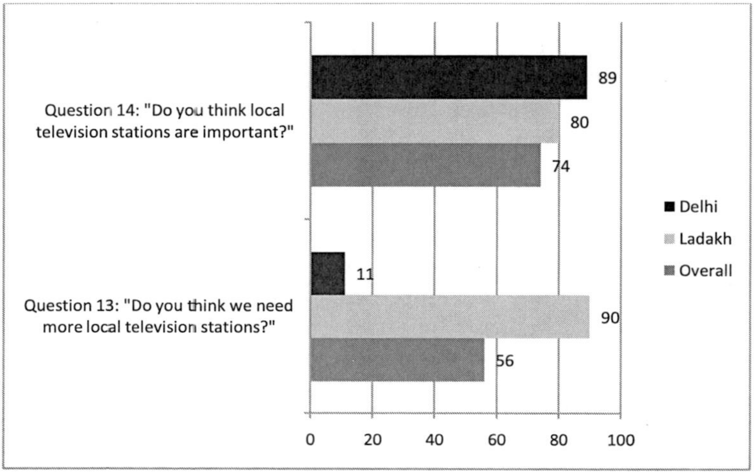

Figure 46: Percentage of people answering "Yes" to each of these questions, by region as well as overall.

The gap between Delhi residents' perceptions of the importance of local television and the need for more channels supports the idea that local stations in Delhi are not living up to expectations. As mentioned earlier, Delhi is one of the biggest cities in the India and the national capital; most of the news covered about Delhi is national level news about the government. Comments in answer to this question suggest ways in which Delhi residents would like to see local stations improve. Some of these are very general, such as that stations should have "more clarity". But others yield more insight. Delhi television viewers are interested in seeing programmes that reflect their lives; as one respondent wrote there was a need for "information customised to our immediate interest area so very relevant", while another one requested that local stations "provide relevant information". Delhi participants are also interested in language issues; one wrote stations should be "language on personal preference based". The survey data suggests that if the local stations cater to a specific locality in Delhi and address their issues then local stations would be more welcome there.

This data also supports the ideas that Ladakh viewers also do not have high expectations of the large national television stations when it comes to getting region-specific news and addressing regional issues. Viewers in Ladakh strongly believe that the local stations can address these issues. Their comments on Question #14 generally agreed that local stations were important. Only one respondent suggested otherwise, writing, "yes to some extant as they will give specific but now the role has been taken by social media such as 'Ladakh in Media' through internet". Language and local news content were the most frequently mentioned issues for the significance of local stations, as respondents wrote "most of the people they can't understand the Urdu or Hindi lang [sic]", that local stations "preserve traditions and promotes usage of language", and that "if the local language is used because it solves the problem of language and everybody educated or not, understands it". A number of the respondents focused on the role of news, writing "native news", "first we should know what is going on in our sorroundings [sic]", and finally, "in order to spread awareness about local issues". The interest in local news is reflected in the interviews of the owners and workers of Kargili local stations, who mention that Kargil is an isolated place and gets little attention in national media. The people of Kargil like watching local stations because they highlight problems and issues faced by Kargilis.

The difference between respondents' attitudes in Delhi and Ladakh is that the Ladakhi participants expect that having local television stations is enough, that if the stations existed they would serve their desired purpose, which the Delhi participants value the idea of local channels but are critical of the reality of offerings available to them. Language is a larger issue in Ladakh, although both groups recognise that offering local language programming is an important role for local stations. People in both areas are interested in watching television programmes, but want to see new programmes that address the issues related to them and their lives, rather than programmes that pretend to represent everyone, or repeat stories with countless television advertisements.

In Question #15 the survey respondents were asked "What kinds of programmes should local television broadcast?" They were given an open comment box answer format that allowed them to answer in their own words. There were 24 responses to this question. A few clear patterns emerged from the text of these answers. While 70.8 per cent of the responses contain mention of news (referring directly to news or current affairs), only 25 per cent of the comments refer to entertainment in any form (movies, reality shows, dances, etc.) as a priority for local stations. Certain words occur multiple times in these comments. 29 per cent of the responses specifically use the terms "social" or "culture/cultural" to refer to types of programmes that they would like to see; almost 17 per cent use the terms "education/educational", while another 17 per cent use the term "development". These indicate some significant themes in Indian's interests in local television stations.

Conclusions

In order to get a more accurate perspective on the role of local television stations in India more extensive research with both online and in-person surveys, covering different parts of India, needs to be done. This survey is significant, however, for multiple reasons. First, it shows how viewers adopt new technologies to watch television shows in India. Second, we can see how there is a complete difference in the understandings of local television stations in different parts of India.

Even though television is still the number one device to watch television shows more and more people in India are slowly moving towards newer technologies to watch news and shows. In remote areas like Ladakh more people are using computers and internet for their news and information due to the convenience of these technologies, and in spite of the cost. People in big cities like Delhi are using more advanced and expensive technologies such as smart phones and tablets to view their news and other programmes.

Even though a majority of participants believe that local television stations can be a great medium for educating and informing the local communities not all feel the same way about how they are actually used. Urban Delhi residents have very low expectations for local television from their experience with television stations that do not reflect news specific to them; as speakers of the majority languages they also do not have language concerns that would cause them to look for alternative stations. In contrast Ladakhi participants, a majority of whom are from Leh, believe that local television stations can preserve culture and bring true news; however since Leh does not have locally run television stations no participant could give an example of a local station that doing that.

In general participants believe that local television should show programmes in the local language, and language seems to be an important feature for conceptualizing a station as local, but there are different viewpoints about defining local television stations. Survey respondents list national and international channels as local television stations, showing that the concept of a local television station, particularly when presented in English, may not be clear to all participants.

Chapter - 6

Balancing the Global and Local

During interviews with television viewers in Kargil I was told multiple times that one of the main reasons most people in Kargil want cable connections is to watch local television stations, because this is the only way the people of Kargil can watch local news daily. As one viewer said in interview, "[w]hatever functions happen during the day, they will record during the day and broadcast during the evening. They don't show this on national news. This is completely locally oriented".

From the perspective of those producing the programmes for Kargili stations, a major motivating theme in the interviews was the idea of connecting Kargil to other places. As one journalist working at television station explained,

> ...there were no local television channels. There were few local newspapers. The national and international television did not cover Kargil because it is a remote area. Geographically in winter Kargil is cut off from the rest of the world for six months and also in terms of media we had no connection with world. Our main focus was to connect Kargil with other parts of the world.

Somehow these two interests, that in focusing in on the local and that of connecting the local outwards to the national and global, have combined to produce a successful media approach for the Kargili stations. The popularity of these stations is such that in many villages of Kargil where there is no cable connection, viewers ask for DVD copies of these programmes. This type of popularity for local television stations in not common in many other parts of India—as demonstrated earlier though the historical studies and my surveys— where many local stations in other areas are considered substandard, have closed, or are now run by larger transnational television corporations. In this research study I have tried to understand the role of local television stations in Kargil India, and why it is popular in Kargil. I have asked, is the success of local media in Kargil a result of fulfilling the needs and desires of the local community in a way that larger national and transnational media outlets fail to do?

This question is worth exploring for several reasons, many listed earlier in the introduction. As I have engaged in my research I have found other reasons why this is a significant contribution to the field of communications. I hope that the information collected from this research study will add something to knowledge in the communications field about the impact of local media, in particular local television, and also that my case study will allow scholars to examine whether the previously claimed roles of local television are universal or not. To specifically understand the role of local media in Kargil I used many different methods and sources, which included census data, interviews, media content analysis, text analysis, digital ethnography, and a survey. Drawing together a number of different sources on media in Kargil has been very helpful for addressing the problem that there is little published about media specifically in Kargil, and to get a full picture how these stations function.

One of those sources, the Census of India data, has helped to show some significant patterns in media in northern Indian media access. The Census of India data demonstrates how media access has rapidly changed in Kargil in recent years. It provides proof against the myths of remote places and their access to new communications technologies;

geographical remoteness alone did not become a major factor for blocking newer technologies from reaching Kargil and from Kargilis adopting these technologies quickly.

In order to better understand the role of local media in general I have looked at the work of different scholars who have contributed to this field and reconstructed the general theoretical background that has been used to explain the study of local media. As mentioned in my earlier chapters a choice of local language use has frequently been associated with local media. Yet, while language plays an important role in increasing the viewership of local media in India, many of the language channels are not always indigenously produced and local languages were not always used in local Kargili television stations.

My research is focused on a small part of India and in many ways significant to understand the role local media plays in remote areas, however broader research is needed from other parts of India to get a more accurate perspective on the role of local television stations in India in general. I would also like to pursue the role of the local community further in future studies, to see what specific contributions the local community can make to the success of a local television channel.

Meeting the Needs of a Community

Does the success of local media actually depend upon whether local media stations meet the needs of a community in ways that larger, transnational stations do not? In order to answer this question completely it is useful to break it down into two separate components: (a) what larger media outlets fail to do for Kargilis, and (2) what the Kargili local stations actually succeed in doing.

The first point about the failure of larger media outlets in Kargil is more generally about the failure of global media in local communities. In Chapter One I wrote about scholars who argue that people choose local media because large national and transnational media often ignore local news unless it is something that requires national or international attention; the First People of Canada television stations and communities were used as an example. Community television is seen as an exception to these corporate television models. In my research it is clear that the contents from national and international television stations have little or nothing to do with Kargil. The population of Kargil is very small, with little purchasing power, so corporations have no interest or reason to start a television station in Kargil. Even the Government of India has not yet opened a local broadcasting studio of Doordarshan in Kargil, although they have one in the Leh region of Ladakh. I was told by all the owners of the local stations in Kargil that the main reason for opening a television station was to highlight the problems and issues faced by Kargilis in this remote part of the world that is often ignored by national and international news organisations. In the survey participants emphasise that large stations repeat the same stories with limitless advertisements and that their content does not reflect the common people. Survey respondents in small towns have higher expectations from local stations as compared to viewers from big cities, whose needs may be met more by the non-local stations in both content and language.

However, the assumption that community television is a mechanism that stays outside the corporate vision is not always true in case of India. This was reflected in the survey data where multiple participants named national and international television stations as local. The respondents named these stations due to the localised broadcasting content and local language shows provided by some of these national and transnational stations. Investments from big media corporations in the local media were also mentioned.

Kargili stations do provide a local answer to the issues of national and transnational media, as well as corporate control. Local stations like the Kargili ones are not affiliated with any outside organisation or corporation, and are very popular in their local communities because of content specific to the region. The content is a form of advocacy for the region; in interviews viewers mentioned that these stations help present public grievances to authorities, who often are non-locals. Thus, those who work at these stations are media activists; the producers of news in Kargili stations stressed in interview that they look at themselves as spokespersons of the community. Not only the contents of the stations' show reflect this; even the graphics that emphasise both Kargil as a region and the world as a whole send a message about the Kargil stations' roles as links between Kargil and other places. In the survey people in the Leh region of Ladakh, who see what is happening in Kargil, reported wanting more local stations, in spite of the fact that they have a national channel with local language and content, because it is a way to get local news and local advocacy. This was not universal though, as respondents in other parts of India did not.

The use of multiple languages in one programme is a mechanism in Kargili media that is outside the convention associated with local language use in non-local stations. When national and transnational channels present local languages it is in a simple form, for example, Ladakhi news in Ladakhi on DDK Leh. In contrast in the Kargili media context the people of Kargil's local language does not serve simply as a form of basic communication or symbol of the local region. Language in Kargili media is playing multiple roles. The use of non-local languages, alternated with multiple local languages, allows the Kargili television producers to frame the narrative in a certain way, gives the diverse Kargilis a united voice, and provides an access to address their problems to authorities who do not speak local languages. Journalists from Kargil have mentioned that local media came into existence primarily as a medium to address the unprecedented difficulties face by Kargilis to the authorities; the use of multiple languages in Kargili media provides a bridge between these groups.

Kargili local television stations have adopted global media technologies for disseminating their programmes, but at the same time have changed some of the television convention to feed their needs and expectations of local viewers. Lack of resources have made Kargili station owners into innovators, they are constantly looking for cheap and reliable technologies to send their news and programmes out to their viewers. By using mobile apps like WhatsApp Kargili television stations can reach out to viewers for purposes other than simply telling about the news, such as engaging audiences in developing news stories, presenting select versions of national and international news, receiving feedback, and allowing community contributions to their stories. WhatsApp groups can engage multiple subcultures of the audience, and news is often shared between groups that have been organised around specific issues and identities. The programmes of these Kargili stations are intersections between different screens such as televisions, computers, and mobile phones. These intersections allow Kargili viewers to be critical media consumers who not only comment on the news, but have discussions about the ways in which the news is shared.

Directions for Future Research

There are many possibilities for follow-up on this study that would provide a good direction for future studies. Some of these could be applied studies in areas that need to be better understood to help communities and activists. A majority of the scholars who have written about local television stations argue that local television was started with the intention of community empowerment, and as a medium for local news and information which will also help in connecting people beyond local communities. Looking at the research done in different parts of the world on local television stations, and the challenges faced by the Kargili stations, it occurs to me that there is not a check list to run a local television station. There are many stories of failure and success of local television stations; each case is different. Some sort of comparative study that brought this information together would be helpful to activists interested in developing their own stations. In these future studies there should be a focus on the patterns of failure and success for local television stations in different parts of the world. This would help the programme producers to focus on people's needs and expectations better and also help to map out how community members can contribute to the stations.

In future academic research on these subjects I think an in-depth study of viewership would be helpful to better understand the role of local television stations. My survey results suggested that an expanded survey on viewers of local television stations that focuses on specific geographic areas of interest could help us to better understand community television. During my research I have learned some interesting things about the local television use of technologies, particularly WhatsApp. Very few studies have been done about the role of messaging apps in different communities, and I have not seen any works on the role of WhatsApp in media contexts. Many more studies could therefore be done on this topic. I would like to investigate whether other media outlets are using social messaging apps, and in what ways. Another specific line of inquiry that would be interesting to pursue is the role of WhatsApp in meeting the needs of different subcultures. During the end of my research I learned that each station runs multiple WhatsApp groups, and that these groups are designed for different sections of the community such as students, women, and people interested in religion. This came up at the end of my work, and because of time limitations I was not able to do research on these different groups. A focus on WhatsApp subcultures would help us to learn more about the use of new technologies by local media, and what local television stations that use these technologies—such as those in Kargil—have to offer to communities of interest in today's global media.

Adapting to Global Technologies

The story of Kargili local stations is a combination of both a local and global one. Two decades ago even someone with a substantial sum of money would have never thought of opening a television station in Kargil—the technology was not available in Kargil and the need was never even considered. As the technology changed, and became more available, more Kargilis saw a need for local stations. Some Kargilis took the matters in their own hands, getting knowledge and experience in the field of media by receiving an education outside of Ladakh and going to work for reputed national and transnational television stations. These experienced Kargili media persons then returned to contribute something to their community by opening local television stations. They had learned from the global media, and used global technologies to create local programmes. These stations began with basic programme formatting and used cable providers for telecasting programmes; however these limited resources did not stop them from finding new ways to send their programmes to local audiences, as well as a small global viewership too.

Owners and producers of the Kargili local stations continue to find new ways to use novel technologies that can serve and benefit the local communities. The station programmes are becoming more complex, with formatting and graphics that resemble those of international television programmes, yet at the same time they are keeping the contents local. Use of apps like WhatsApp allows for news that is participatory and has a compelling narrative. The localisation of global technologies by these stations occurs in ways that serve their purposes and meet present needs. Adopting new technologies, however, does not mean that local television stations in Kargil have any power or control over these technologies and there is no surety about how long these solutions will last. Adopting newer technologies is not the only issue that these local stations in Kargil are facing; to be more efficient and fulfill the needs of local communities they also have to shape their programmes so that they will fit into a fast-moving system of media convergence where consumers play a significant role. The Kargili local stations are firmly located within Appadurai's mediascape, larger media discourses shaped by the forces of globalisation, but may have limited power there.

As discussed earlier in this book Schirato and Webb's idea of contemporary globalisation is that it is a set of discourses, practices, and relations that are informed by power relations, practices, and technologies that have shaped the modern world (Schirato and Webb, 2003). The complexity of these discourses, practices, and relations can be seen in the Kargil case. The forces of globalisation have not only exposed places like Kargil to new technologies, but it has given them an opportunity to participate in new discourses, to create a local media that is being used to address the problems of the local community. The localisation of global technology has benefited local media, but this may be a temporary effect of globalisation.

The future for these Kargili local television stations—with limited resources, unreliable technologies and competition from national and transnational television corporations—will be challenging, but up to this time these owners and producers have faced many of these same odds and survived. I think the success and survival of these stations will depend squarely on the role of their viewers. While these television station owners and journalists are working as activists, more community involvement is necessary. The community should be involved in more stages of the media process than the distribution of news and participation in the media on WhatsApp; I was not told by any of those interviewed that the community plays any role in the functioning these stations and production of programmes. Community involvement will necessitate, and encourage, further consideration of the subcultures of Kargili audiences, allowing the local stations the opportunity to better recognise the diversity of identities and interest groups within the region. Furthermore if these stations are to grown it must be in quality rather than quantity; I do not see a need for more than three local stations in a small place like Kargil.

The future of Kargili local media and other similar media outlets is very uncertain; a small change in communication technologies can disturb their whole process. There is, however, a great deal of potential in this media. If local media such as that in Kargil continues to grow and innovate with new technologies they have the potential to impact change in media in other parts of the world. Their successes could become a template for local media in other parts of the world, shaping Appadurai's mediascape and making it a more truly global media.

Bibliography

Al Noor News Ladakh (Producer). (2013). Episode 22 Umeed Ki Kirn. Retrieved from https://www.youtube.com/watch?v=1j3vlwRZ5XQ

Al Noor News Ladakh (Producer). (2014a). Face to Face Talk with Thupten Tsewang. Retrieved from http://youtu.be/L6jgGPjOPrc

Al Noor News Ladakh. (2014b). Munshi Habibullah Mission School Kargil Commercial.

Al Noor News Ladakh. (2014c). The Zojilla Issue & The Kargili Peoples problem (May 11, 2014 ed.).

Al Noor News Ladakh (Producer). (2015a). Aawam ke Aawaz: Sharchey Village Boycott Comming Assembly Elections. Retrieved from https://www.youtube.com/watch?v=76S4aEZ17eI

Al Noor News Ladakh. (2015b). Al Noor News Network from http://www.alnoornews.in/

Al Noor News Ladakh (Producer). (2015c). Breaking News.

Al Noor News Ladakh (Producer). (2015d). Comment.

Al Noor News Ladakh (Producer). (2015e). Latest Update of Zojila Pass.

Appadurai, A. (1990). Disjuncture and Difference in the Global Cultural Economy. *Public Culture, 2*, 1-24.

Asthana, S. (2013). Broadcasting, Space, and Sovereignty in India, *Media, Culture & Society, 35*, 516-534.

Baltruschat, D. (2004). Television and Canada's Aboriginal Communities: Seeking Opportunities through Traditional

Storytelling and Digital Technologies. *Canadian Journal of Communication, 29*(1), 47-59.

Bhalla, A., James, D., and Stevens, Y. (1984). Chapter 16. India's Rural Educational Television Broadcasting via Satellites, *Blending of New and Traditional Technologies-Case Studies*: Tycooly Int.

Bonner, A. (1959, October). India's Masses: the Public That Can't Be Reached. *The Atlantic Montly*.

Business Today. (2014). WhatsApp to be free for Indian users: Report. from http://businesstoday.intoday.in/story/whatsapp-indian-users-hangouts-snapchat-we-chat-line-skype/1/212182.html

Centre, N. I. (2015).

Chatterjee, A. N. (2012). Inequalities in the Public Sphere: Emergence of Community Television in India. *Asian Ethnicity, 13* (3), 229-250.

Chen, W., Funk, M., Straubhaar, J., and Spence, J. (2013). Still Relevant? An Audience Analysis of Public and Government Access Channels. *Journal of Broadcasting & Electronic Media, 57*(3), 263-281.

Choudhari, P. (2014). Study on effectiveness of communication amongst members at department of orthopedics surgery unit 3 using smartphone and mobile WhatsApp. *International Surgery Journal.*

Church, K., and de Oliveira, R. (2013). *What's up with WhatsApp? Comparing Mobile Instant Messaging Behaviors with Traditional SMS.* Paper presented at the Mobile HCI 2013 - Collaboration and Communication, Munich, Germany.

District Administration Kargil, L. (2015). A brief history of Kargil. from http://kargil.gov.in/profile/profile.htm

Durham, M. G., and Kellner, D. M. (2006). *Media and Cultural Studies.* Oxford: Blackwell Publishing.

Editor Kargil Today. (2015, January 18, 2015) *Interview with Hussain Khalo Editor in Chief Kargil Today / Interviewer: A. N. Khan.*

Facebook. (2014). Facebook to Acquire WhatsApp. from http://newsroom.fb.com/news/2014/02/facebook-to-acquire-whatsapp/

Fewkes, J. H. (2006). Trade at the Crossroads of Continents Northern India's Ladakh Region. *Expedition: The Magazine of the University of Pennsylvania Museum of Archaeology and Anthropology, 48,* 48.

Fewkes, J. H. (2009). *Trade and Contemporary Society along the Silk Road: An ethno-history of Ladakh*: Routledge.

Fontevecchia, A. (2014). India's 243 Million Internet Users And The Mobile E-Commerce Revolution. 2015, from http://www.forbes.com/sites/afontevecchia/2014/07/07/indias-massive-e-commerce-opportunity-and-the-explosion-of-mobile/

Ginsburg, F. (1994). Embedded Aesthetics: Creating a Discursive Space for Indigenous Media. *Cultural Anthropology, 9*(3), 365-382.

GlobalWebIndex. (2014a). *15 Trends for 2015.*

GlobalWebIndex. (2014b). *Global Web Index November 2014.*

Gov. of India, M. o. H. A. (2001). Census of India 2001.

Gov. of India, M. o. H. A. (2011). Census of India 2011.

Hanusch, F. (2013). Charting a Theoretical Framework for Examining Indigenous Journalism Culture. *Media International Australia Incorporating Culture and Policy, 149*, 82.

Higgins, J. W. (1999). Community Television and the Vision of Media Literacy, Social Action, and Empowerment. *Journal of Broadcasting & Electronic Media, 43*(4), 624-644.

Hussain, N. (2015). *Interview with Nasir Hussain S TV Ladakh / Interviewer: A. N. Khan.*

Hussain, S. (2015, February 7, 2015) *Interview with Sajjad Hussain Works for Sahar Urdu TV (correspondent for Ladakh region) / Interviewer: A. N. Khan.*

Jenkins, H. (2006). *Convergence Culture: Where Old and New Media Collide.* New York: New York University Press.

Jenkins, J. (2014). *Global Englishes: A Resource Book for Students* (Vol. 2015): Routledge.

Kargil Today (Producer). (2013). KT Drass Winter Story. Retrieved from http://youtu.be/z2P-7TML2kc

Kargil Today (Producer). (2015a). KT Flash.

Kargil Today (Producer). (2015b). KT News Headlines, Hosain Ibn Khalo, New Year 2015. Retrieved from https://youtu.be/XlHrfXgUbVA

Khalo, H. (2015, 1/18/2015). *Interview with Hussain Khalo Kargil Today / Interviewer: A. N. Khan.*

Kim, E. (2015). WhatsApp's Insane Growth Continues: 100 Million New Users in 4 Months. from http://www.businessinsider.in/WhatsApps-Insane-Growth-Continues

King, D. L., and Mele, C. (1999). Making Public Access Television: Community Participation, Media Literacy and the Public Sphere. *Journal of Broadcasting & Electronic Media, 43*(4), 603-623.

Ladakhi, B. H. (2015, 1/17/2015) *Interview with Basharat Hussain Ladakhi / Interviewer: A. N. Khan.*

Lewis, P. M. (2009). Ethnologue: Languages of the World (Online Database). Retrieved May 2nd, 2015, from SIL International http://www.ethnologue.com

Lone, M. A. (2013). Ladakh: Society, people and Place: A Sociological Outlook. *Acme International Journal of Multidisciplinary Research, 1*(5), 112-119.

Mankekar, P. (1999). *Screening Culture, Viewing Politics: An Ethnography of Television, Womanhood, and Nation in Postcolonial India*. London: Duke University Press.

McChesney, R. W. (2001). Global Media, Neoliberalism, and Imperialism. *Monthly Review Mar ProQuest Social Sciences Premium Collection, 52*(10), 1-19.

McDowell, S. D. (1997). Globalisation and Policy Choice: Television and Audiovisual Services Policies in India. *Media Culture Society, 19*(2), 151-172.

Meadows, M. (2009). Electronic Dreaming Tracks: Indigenous Community Broadcasting in Australia. *Development in Practice, 19*(4), 514-524.

Morup, T. (2002). Leh Radio Station Gutted in Devestating Fire. *International Association for Ladakh Studies Newsletter,* 7.

Noor Ul Islam. (2015a, 1/5/2015). *Interview with Noor Ul Islam / Interviewer: A. N. Khan.*

Noor Ul Islam. (2015b). *Interview with Noor Ul Islam Al Noor News Ladakh / Interviewer: A. N. Khan.*

O'Hara, K., Massimi, M., Harper, R., Rubens, S., and Morris, J. (2014). *Everyday Dwelling with WhatsApp.* Paper presented at the Computer Supported Cooperative Work 2014, Baltimore, MD.

Oswald, K., and Packer, J. (2011). Flow and Mobile Media Broadcast Fixity to Digital Fluidity. In J. Packer and S. B. C. Wiley (Eds.), *Communication Matters: Materialist Approaches to Media, Mobility and Networks.* London: Routledge.

Paldan, T. (2002). *Languages Change: From Preclassical Tibetan to Modern Spoken Ladakhi.* Paper presented at the 8th Himalayan Languages Symposium, Berne, Switzerland.

Rambe, P., and Chipunza, C. (2013). *Using mobile devices to leverage student access to collaboratively-generated resources: A case of WhatsApp instant messaging at a South African University.* Paper presented at the International Conference on Advanced Information and Communication Technology for Education (ICAICTE, 2013).

Roth, L. (2000). Bypassing of Borders and Building of Bridges: Steps in the Construction of the Aboriginal Peoples Television Network in Canada. *International Communication Gazette, 62*(3-4), 251-269.

Roy, A. (2008). Bringing up TV: Popular Culture and the Developmental Modern in India. *South Asian Popular Culture, 6*(1), 29-43.

S TV Ladakh. (2014). Winter Folk Festival at Mulbek In Kargil Org-by-by Culture and Languages Academy.

S TV Ladakh. (2015a). News.

S TV Ladakh (Producer). (2015b). News Headlines.

Sawchuk, K., Crow, B., and Longford, M. (2010). Introduction. In B. Crow, M. Longford, and K. Sawchuk (Eds.), *The Wireless Spectrum: The Politics, Practices, and Poetics of Mobile Media* (pp. 1-13). Toronto: University of Toronto.

Schirato, T., and Webb, J. (2003). *Understanding Globalisation.* London: SAGE Publication Ltd.

Shambare, R. (2014). The Adoption of WhatsApp: Breaking the Vicious Cycle of Technological Poverty in South Africa. *Journal of Economics and Behavioral Studies, 6*(7), 542-550.

Shotopa, A. A. (2015). *Interview with Anayat Ali Shotopa/ Interviewer: A. N. Khan.*

Sinclair, J. (2005). Globalisation and Grassroots: Local Cable Television Operators and their Household Subscribers in India. *Media Asia, 32*(2), 69-77.

Singhal, A., Doshi, J. K., Rogers, E. M., and Rahman, S. A. (1988). The Diffusion of Television. *Media Asia, 15*(4), 222-229.

SurveyMonkey. (2015). About us.

Tawiah, Y. S., Nondzor, H. E., and Alhaji, A. (2014). Usage of WhatsApp and Voice Calls (Phone Call): Preference of Polytechnic Students in Ghana. *Science Journal of Business and Management, 2*(4), 103-108.

Thomas, P. (2014). Communication and Global Power Shifts: The Ambivalent State and the Media in India: Between Corporate Compulsions and the Public Interest. *International Journal of Communication,* 8.

WhatsApp. (2015). *Whats App We are Social.*

Wilson, S., and Peterson, L. C. (2002). The Anthropology of Online Communities. *Annual Review of Anthropology, 31*, 449-467.

Wired. (2014). You May Not Use WhatsApp, But the Rest of the World Sure Does. from http://www.wired.com/2014/02/whatsapp-rules-rest-world/

Yeboah, J., and Ewur, G. D. (2014). The Impact of Whatsapp Messenger Usage on Students Performance in Tertiary Institutions in Ghana. *Journal of Education and Practice, 5*(6), 157-164.

Zaidi, N. H. (2015a, 1/20/2015). *Interview with Nasir Hussain / Interviewer: A. N. Khan.*

Zaidi, N. H. (Producer). (2015b). Winter Game in Kargil. Retrieved from https://youtu.be/uKjNAmsM-oU

Zivin, J. (1998). The Imagined Reign of the Iron Lecturer: Village Broadcasting in Colonial India. *Modern Asian Studies, 32*(3), 717-738.

Index

G

H

I

J

K

L

N

P

R

S

T

U

W

Y